CW01270774

AMONG THESE DARK SATANIC MILLS

BRITAIN'S INDUSTRIAL HERITAGE Volume 4

written and photographed by
John Hannavy

First published in 2022

Text, photography, digital image restorations and design, copyright © 2022 John Hannavy.
www.johnhannavy.co.uk

All rights reserved. Apart from any fair dealing for the purpose of private study, research, criticism or review, as permitted under the Copyright, Designs and Patents Act, 1988, no part of this publication may be reproduced, stored in a retrieval system, or transmitted in any form or by any means, electronic, electrical, chemical, mechanical, optical, photocopying, recording or otherwise, without the prior written permission of the copyright owner. Enquiries should be addressed to the Publishers.

Every attempt has been made by the author and publisher to secure the appropriate permissions for materials reproduced in this book. If there has been any oversight we will be happy to rectify the situation and a written submission should be made to the Publishers.

A CIP catalogue record for this book is available from the British Library.

John Hannavy has asserted his right under the Copyright, Designs and Patents Act 1988 to be identified as the author of this book.

ISBN: 978 0 85710 127 3

PiXZ Books
Halsgrove House, Ryelands Business Park,
Bagley Road, Wellington,
Somerset TA21 9PZ
Tel: 01823 653777
Fax: 01823 216796
email: sales@halsgrove.com

An imprint of Halstar Ltd, part of the Halsgrove group of companies. Information on all Halsgrove titles is available at: www.halsgrove.com

Printed and bound in India by
Parksons Graphics

COVER IMAGE
The Power Hall in Manchester's Museum of Science & Industries is now home to some of the region's finest mill and factory engines. This 1000hp Galloway engine, built in 1926, was the last large steam engine to be installed in a British mill.

TITLE PAGE IMAGE
One of the restored 1886 Gimson steam engines which powered Claymills Pumping Station in Derbyshire. Shut down in 1971 – having given way to electricity – three of the engines have since been restored and are regularly steamed for visitors. Work is on-going on the fourth.

CONTENTS PAGE IMAGE
The working machine shop at the Amberley Museum & Heritage Centre in West Sussex.

All the modern photographs in this book are © the author except the following – p64 courtesy of the Museum of Bath at Work; p49 top © Duncan Hannavy
All Victorian and Edwardian images are © John Hannavy Image Library.

By the same author, also published by PiXZ:
- EDWARDIAN MINING IN OLD POSTCARDS
- EDWARDIAN RAILWAYS IN POSTCARDS
- PRESERVED STEAM-POWERED MACHINES
- THE ONCE-UBIQUITOUS PADDLE-STEAMER
- BRITAIN'S INDUSTRIAL HERITAGE
- OUR INDUSTRIAL PAST - *Britain's Industrial Heritage 2*
- INDUSTRIES WHICH MADE BRITAIN TRIUMPH - *Britain's Industrial Heritage 3*

CONTENTS

PREFACE 5

INTRODUCTION 7

ABOUT TIME 25

THE RISE AND DEMISE OF THE MILL 37

SICKLES, NEEDLES AND NAILS 59

A LUST FOR LIME 75

A NATION OF SHOPKEEPERS 93

PHOTOGRAPHING THE INDUSTRIAL
WORLD 107

GAZETTEER 125

INDEX 143

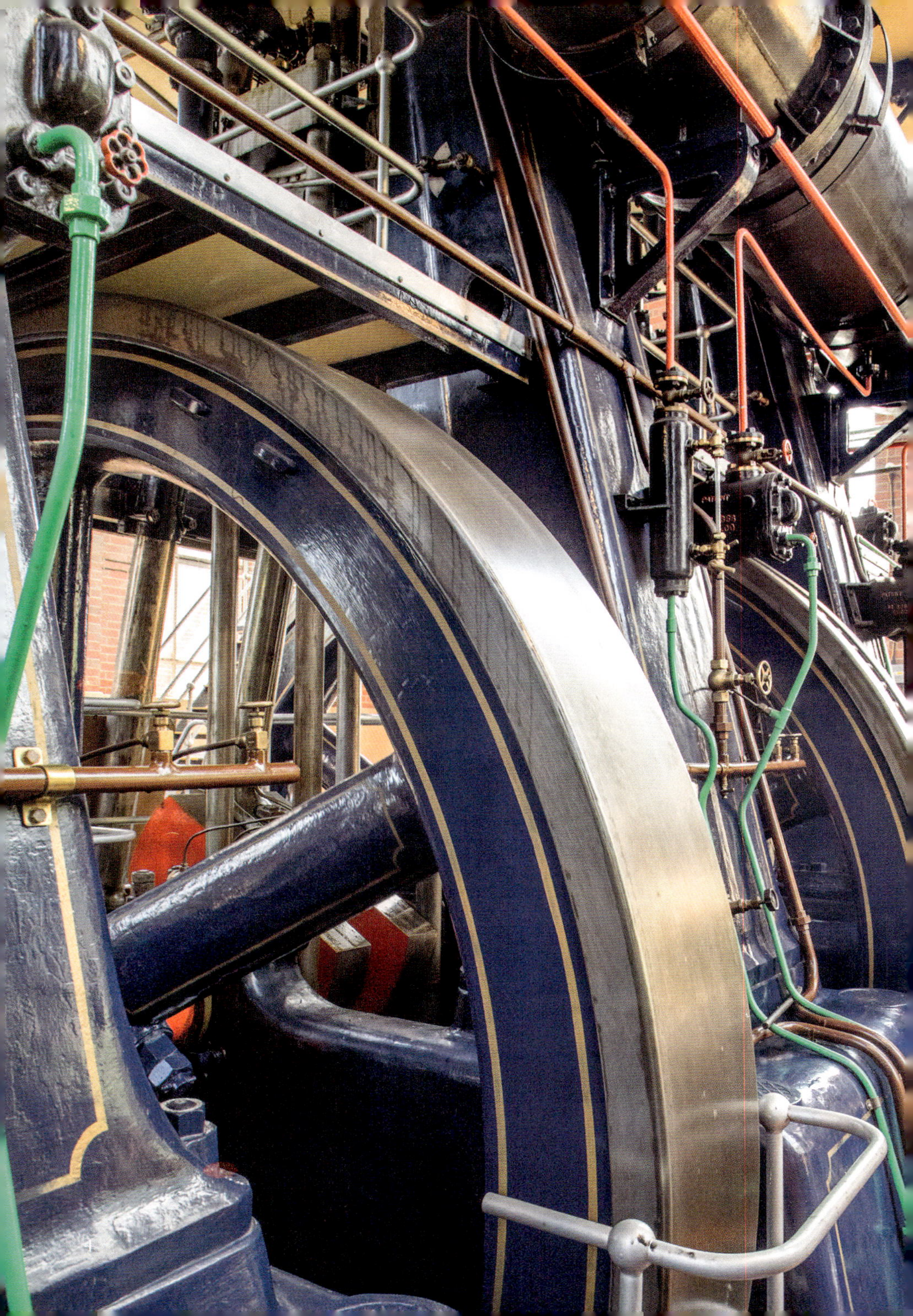

PREFACE

THIS FOURTH LOOK at aspects of Britain's long, proud industrial heritage is, like the three earlier books in this series, an eclectic bringing together of industries which, in most cases, are kept alive today on heritage sites so that we can see – and enjoy – a glimpse of a long-lost past. Like the earlier books, a thematic approach has been used to explore the legacy of past generations, and along the way I have once again come face to face with machinery and processes which I had never seen before.

As with all of my books, I am indebted to the many experts and volunteers at industrial sites, museums and libraries who have welcomed me, given me access to their collections, and shared their immense knowledge with me.

Without their hard work – and their willingness to let me roam freely with my camera and share briefly in what they do – this final volume in the series just would not have been possible. And thanks – as ever – to Kath, my wife, for her continuing support and encouragement.

I can only hope you get as much pleasure out of visiting the sites featured in this book as I did – they all depend on us visiting and paying our entrance fees in order to cover their operating costs. So its the proverbial 'win-win' situation – great days out for us while at the same time helping preserve Britain's unique industrial heritage.

John Hannavy 2022

opposite: The massive 1940-built triple-expansion Worthington-Simpson pumping engine at Brede Waterworks in Sussex, was once one of the three 'Giants of Brede' which provided fresh water to Hastings from deep aquifers. It was installed in a new Art Deco engine house when the capacity of the original pair of Tangye engines proved insufficient to meet demand.

below left: The Brede collection now includes many other engines and ancillary equipment telling the story of the water industry. This large Ruston engine occupies part of the space where one of the pair of large Tangye pumping engines once stood. The second of the pair survives and, like all the other engines on display, is now turned over using compressed air while funds are raised to install a new boiler and return the site to steam.

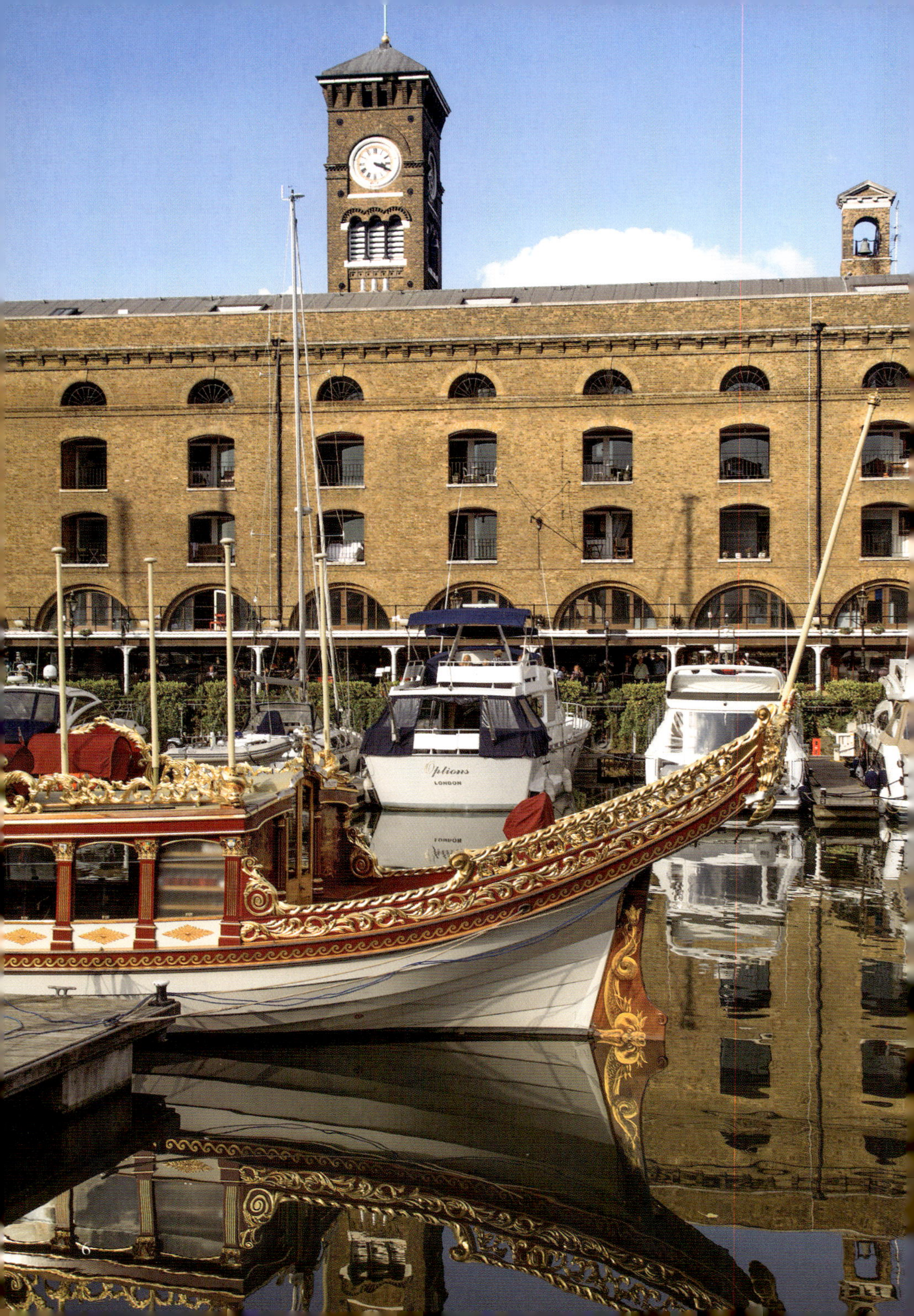
Options
LONDON

INTRODUCTION

THE PHRASE 'AMONG THESE DARK SATANIC MILLS' was coined by William Blake in the early nineteenth century and was first included in his poem *And Did Those Feet in Ancient Time* – part of the Preface to his epic poem *Milton*. Today, set to music by Sir Hubert Parry in 1916, it is best known as *Jerusalem*.

The phrase, which has become widely adopted as a metaphor for the appalling working conditions of the Industrial Revolution – and the impact which large mills and factories had on the lives of those whose smaller businesses were squeezed out of existence – may not have been written with that intention in mind at all. Rather it is believed by many to have been a protest against the established churches which used the imposition of conformity as a means of enslaving the working classes.

Whichever is the true origin, the phrase has long since become a metaphor for the colossal impact which large factories had on the lives of the majority of the population.

While the great industries – great both in terms of their importance and their scale – inspire awe and wonder when we encounter the surviving relics of them, they were all

opposite page: Photographed in 2016, Thomas Telford's great warehouses in St Catherine's Dock, London – now apartments – look out over *Gloriana*, the beautiful barge hand-built to mark the Queen's Diamond Jubilee in 2012.

below: Every large manufacturing plant – such as the great Westinghouse factory in Manchester's Trafford Park seen here in a 1905 postcard – depended upon hundreds of smaller industries employing thousands of people further down the supply chain.

AMONG THESE DARK SATANIC MILLS

above: The headframe at Caphouse Colliery in Yorkshire, now home to the National Mining Museum, England. Millions of tons of coal were burned annually to drive Britain's thousands of mills and factories.

above right: Detail from the great Worth Mackenzie steam engine which drove the pumps at Hereford Waterworks.

right: Visitors to Coleham Pumping Station in Shrewsbury watch both their Renshaw rotative beam engines operating.

dependent upon the countless smaller, but equally important, industries which made them possible. It is those supporting industries with which this volume largely concerns itself – everything from making the nails which built houses and factories, the needles which sewed Britain's clothes, and the timepieces which regulated working lives.

There was, in Victorian and Edwardian times, an enormous gulf between the ever brighter shop windows which graced high streets in every town, and the appalling conditions under which the people who manufactured those everyday goods lived and worked – not dissimilar to the gulf between today's bright and colourful department stores and the sweat-shops in the Far East where many of our clothes and household goods are now made.

Britain may have moved a long way towards better living and working conditions for its own workforce, but in many parts of the world, what we might call Victorian practices still prevail in order to keep us supplied with inexpensive clothes and household goods.

Throughout Britain, many of the great mills and factories which powered the growth of both industry and commerce have been preserved and lovingly restored for us to visit and enjoy. OK, so we will never see them, hear them, or smell them at their worst – 'Health & Safety' regulations preclude that – but at least we can get a taste of the conditions under which our predecessors worked.

top left: Jacquard looms introduced semi-automation to the weaving industry.

top right: Gas engines replaced coal as a fuel in many industrial complexes – this example is now in the Hereford Waterworks Museum Collection.

above: James Watt, the father of steam.

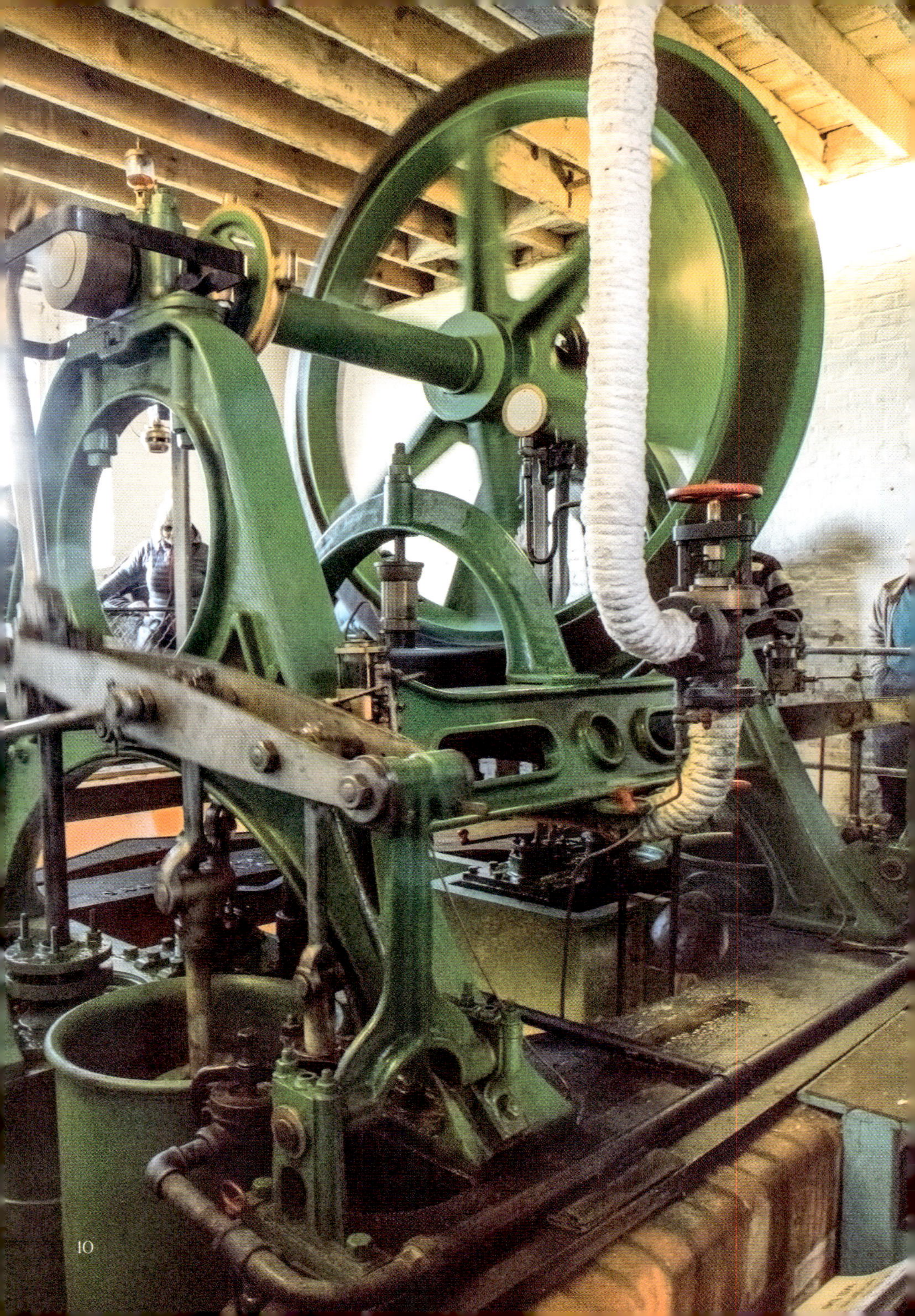

INTRODUCTION

We can, however, get a sense of the common core of engineering innovations which made those mills, factories and pumping stations work, and along the way understand something of the industrial ingenuity which created them.

opposite page: The huge Easton Amos Land Drainage Machine at Westonzoyland which helped drain the Somerset Levels.

above left: The engine house shrouded in steam as the great engine is prepared for use.

above right: Steam powered just about everything — this is a steam-powered milk bottle-washing machine.

left: The steam winch which once hauled milk wagons into Hemyock Dairy near Wellington, Somerset.

11

12

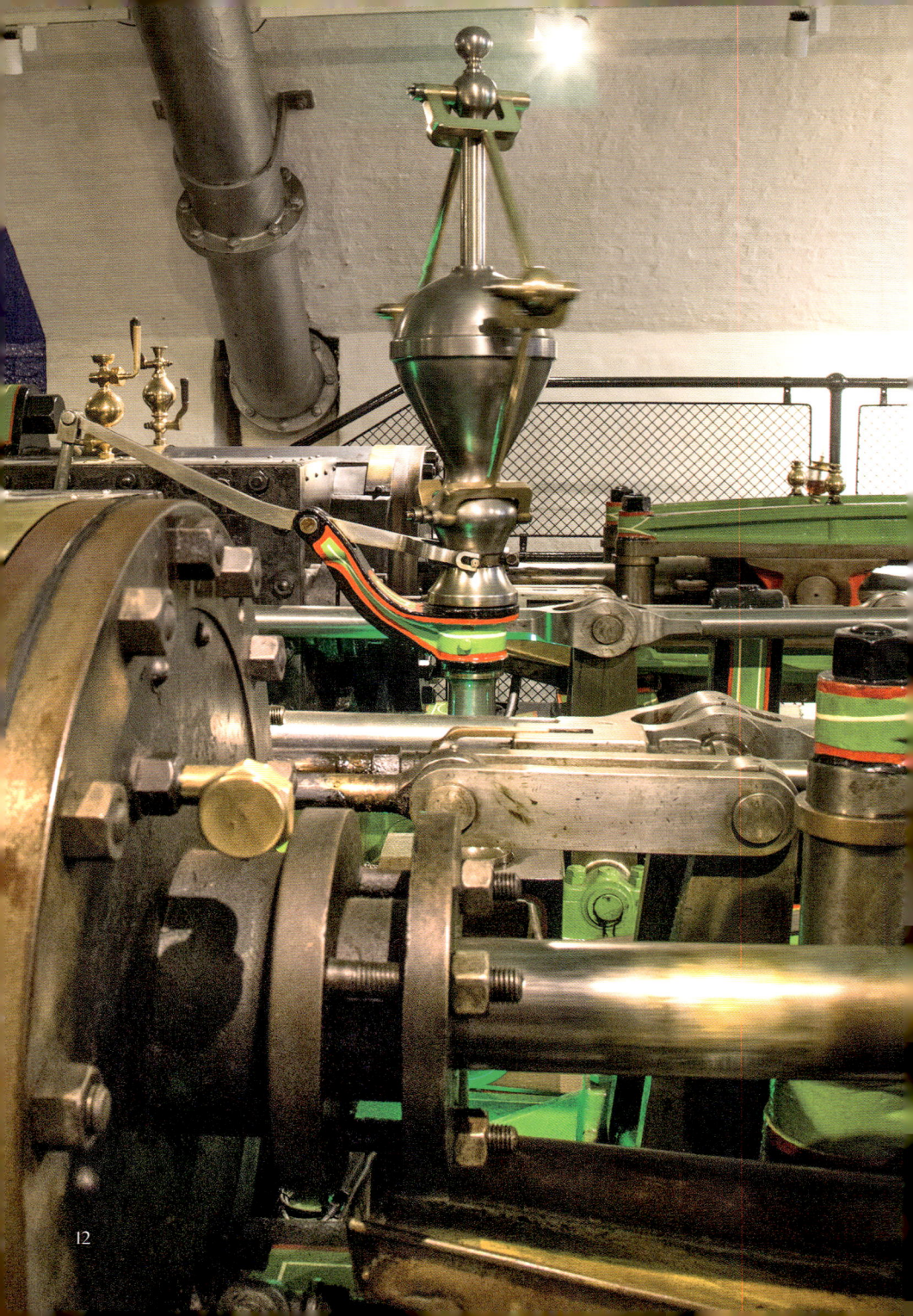

INTRODUCTION

James Watt's contribution to the evolution of steam power is celebrated the world over, despite the fact that many of his 'inventions' ought really to be ascribed to others. His genius was in bringing together a range of other people's ideas, adding his own pioneering inventions such as the parallel motion system which converted vertical motion to rotative motion, and making them work as a whole.

opposite page: One of the 1893 Armstrong, Mitchell & Co. compound engines which used to power London's Tower Bridge.

above: A 1927 single-cylinder horizontal four-stroke diesel engine with electrical generator, built by the National Gas & Oil Engine Company of Ashton-under-Lyne, now in the Power Hall at Manchester's Museum of Science & Industry.

left: The 2500hp steam engine at Trencherfield Spinning Mill, Wigan. Such machines were precision engineering on a massive scale.

13

right: The boilers at Westonzoyland Pumping Station on the Somerset Levels, built by Fred Danks Ltd of Birmingham.

below: Lancashire boilers at Cefn Coed Colliery near Neath in South Wales. Cefn Coed was the deepest anthracite mine in the world when it was opened by the Amalgamated Anthracite Company in 1926. Coal was first raised in 1930 from seams nearly 800 metres below ground, using a huge winding engine built by the Worsley Mesnes Company Ltd of Wigan. There was a lot of methane in the pit, and the boilers were later converted to burn this gas rather than coal – the coal had a commercial value, the gas did not.

In 1882 the unit of power was named after him, so every time we buy a lightbulb, switch on an electric fire, or define the power of a machine, we talk of 'watts', 'kilowatts' and 'megawatts' without thinking about the word's origin.

At the heart of many of the great engines which were harnessed to power the new factories were Lancashire boilers – a great leap forward in boiler technology dating from the 1840s – in which twin fireboxes gave the boiler-man greater control over the heat and efficiency of the boiler, thus giving his engine-man more control over the engine itself.

INTRODUCTION

Where absolute consistency of engine speed was vital – in spinning and weaving mills for example – even slight deviations would lead to inconsistencies in the thickness of the yarns being spun or the cloth being woven.

That could result in a huge loss of revenue for the mill-owners – with batches of yarn being rejected by their customers –and a consequential loss of wages for the workers who were invariably paid on piecework rates.

Without the steam engine, as Andrew Carnegie rightly pointed out, the country's industrial growth could not have happened, but whatever the benefits of the steam engine – and they were many and essential – the change in working practices which they brought about was colossal.

The result was an underclass who were treated little better than slaves, who worked long hours for meagre wages, and whose children also had to earn their keep by doing those dangerous jobs where an adult's hands were just too big. The cost on young lives was huge.

The unstoppable growth of water and steam-powered mechanisation drove the country's workforce out of their small workshops and home weaving lofts into factories, making the concept of 'going to work' quite distinct from simply 'working'.

The impact of gas lighting, and later electricity, in the factories which grew up across the country changed the natural rhythm of working life from being something one did when there was daylight, to following the shrill summons of the factory whistle which, for most of the year, started the working day before dawn and ended it after dusk.

The individual skill of the craftsman and the individuality of

above: The maker's nameplate on one of Eastney Pumping Station's 1887 beam engines, Southsea.

below: Firing the Robey 'Leviathan' portable engine which now drives the machinery at Westonzoyland. These engines had widespread applications.

above: Carding machines at Stanley Mills in Perthshire. Richard Arkwright was one of the mill's founders, and David Dale – one of the New Lanark pioneers – was involved in its re-construction after a disastrous fire. Stanley village nearby was built in the 1780s to house the mill workers and by 1831 the population had reached around 2000, half of whom worked in the mill.

above right: Workers' cottages and Sunday School – one of the streets in Samuel Greg's model village which he built adjacent to his Quarry Bank Mill at Styal, Cheshire.

right: Stanley Mills and sluice gate – the mill was powered by water from the adjacent River Tay.

his produce was replaced by the uniformity, repeatability and guaranteed precision of factory mass-produced objects. Quality and consistency improved, and the costs of buying everyday objects fell – but in most cases, the working and living conditions of those who worked in those inhospitable factories also fell.

The relationship between the working life and family life of the weaver, for example, changed more than most as he made the forced transition from being self-employed to being an employee.

As anyone who has visited surviving Victorian mills is aware, the conditions under which workers were required to operate, and the risks to which they were daily exposed, were often appalling. Mills and factories were noisy, dangerous and unhealthy places in which to work.

The cost of making Britain the world's most powerful industrial nation was largely borne by the millions of workers who produced its wealth but got little chance to share in it.

There were a few enlightened employers – enlightened by eighteenth and nineteenth century standards, that is – who sought to make living and working conditions for their workers a bit more bearable. Amongst them, Samuel Greg of Quarry Bank Mill in Styal, Cheshire, and David Dale and Robert Owen at New Lanark in Scotland, built model communities in which their employees both lived and worked.

below: Now a World Heritage Site, New Lanark village and mill was the brainchild of David Dale and Robert Owen, who saw the obvious benefits of providing good basic housing for their employees and rudimentary education for their children.

bottom: If a thread broke on a spinning mule, children were used to repair the break. Adults were too large to get inside the moving mechanism without stopping the machine. Children, being much smaller, could crawl underneath the moving frame and carry out repairs as necessary. A moment's loss of concentration or a misjudgment could, however — and often did — result in life-changing injuries. With later vertical ring-spinning machines, that dangerous task was no longer necessary. This spinning frame is regularly used for demonstration purposes in New Lanark Mill.

Some Victorian and Edwardian industries involved appalling working conditions — even when making something as 'clean' as soap. These Valentine postcards from around 1910 show the interior of the Sunlight Soap factory at Port Sunlight in Cheshire. But while conditions on the factory might have been challenging, Lever Brothers, who owned the works, created a model village in which to house their workforce and educate their children.

That approach would later be replicated by William Hesketh Lever and James Darcy Lever at Port Sunlight on the Wirral Peninsula in Cheshire – their workers' village named after their most popular brand of soap – and George and Richard Cadbury, the chocolate pioneers at Bournville in the Midlands.

There were several others who recognised that a more contented workforce was a better workforce, but the majority did little to ameliorate the cultural and social shift which factory working brought about in people's lives.

The soubriquet of the 'Dark Satanic Mill' was quickly earned, widely applied, and difficult to shake off.

In many cases it had been fairly earned. The inside of a cotton mill was notoriously damp and unhealthy – the prevalence of tuberculosis amongst mill girls was high – and the women who graded and sorted coal at the Victorian and Edwardian pithead were often reported as citing health reasons for their preference for the hard outdoor work and grime of the colliery yard over the hot noisy and humid conditions of the mills.

The working conditions inside the country's increasing number of large engineering factories, foundries and assembly shops were no better – and, in the days before any consideration of health and safety, often little short of lethal.

The Factory Inspectorate had been set up as early as 1833 and the Railway Inspectorate in 1840 but, despite progress being made to improve working conditions, accident reports suggest they initially had limited effectiveness.

The role of factory inspectors – and initially there was just a handful of them – was to ensure that any children employed in cotton mills were not below the legal minimum age, and did not work excessive hours – the pressing issue of workplace safety would not be considered for decades.

The first Medical Inspector of Factories, however, was not appointed until 1898, despite a growing body of evidence over the preceding decades that there were

Chocolate giant Cadbury's, whose Bournville factory was in the Midlands, also built a model village to house their workers and take care of their housing, social, educational and moral welfare. Numerous tinted postcards were published celebrating this 'Utopian' approach to progressive and enlightened industrial management.

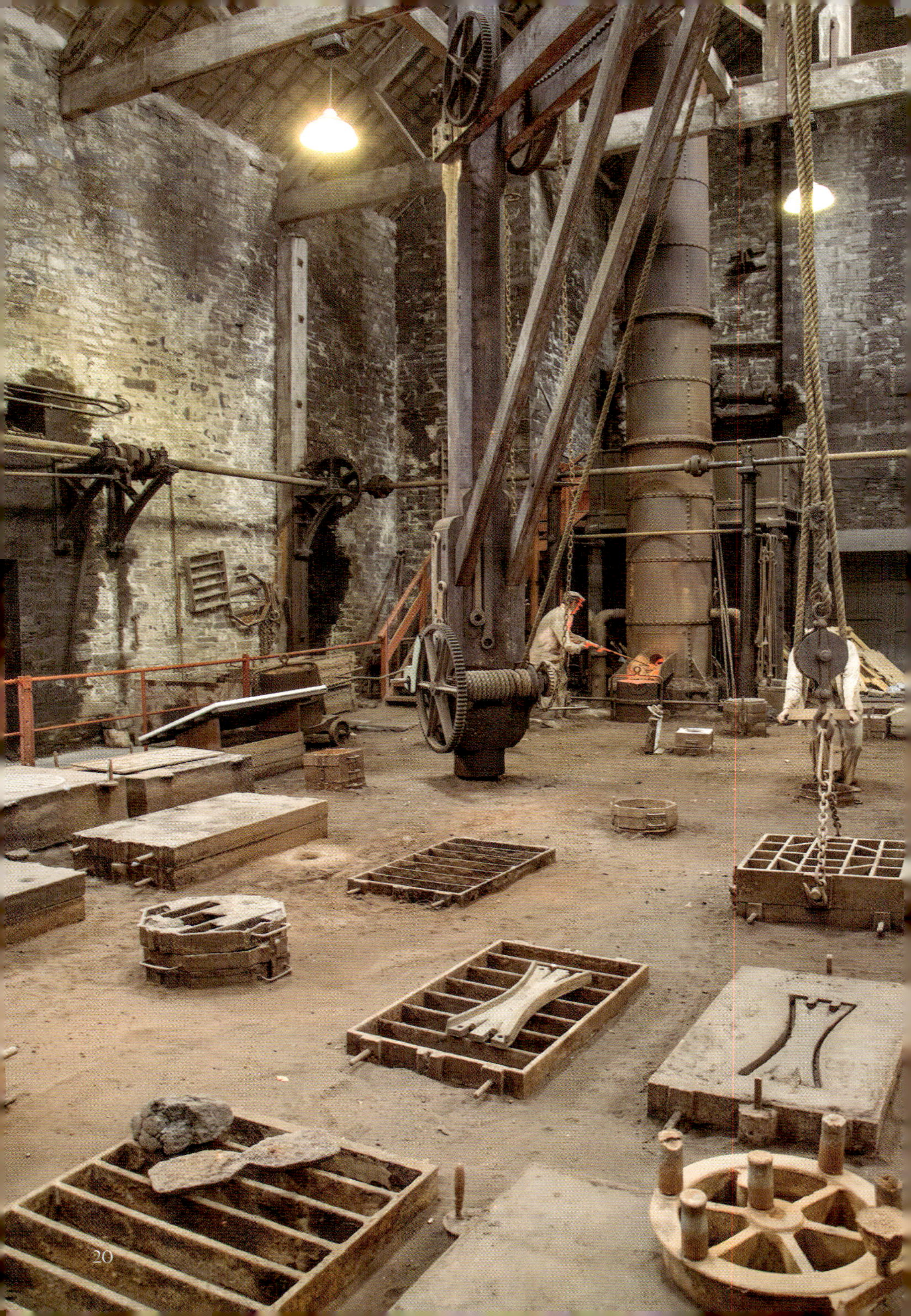

significant health and safety issues. Workers, of course, were in plentiful supply and the pressure to constantly improve and increase output was immense.

The one thing pictures of our heritage sites can't show is any sense of the terrible working conditions, noise and intense heat under which many of our forefathers worked – foundry floors where molten metal was moved around in red hot flasks and poured into moulds; shipyards where red-hot rivets were thrown up to be caught in the riveters' gloved hands. None of that can be recreated for visitors today, but a century and more ago, such things were commonplace.

Mills and factories were just the starting point for Britain's emergence as the greatest industrial power of the age. A complex infrastructure of supply chains and export routes – based on railways and shipping – was key to that success.

The relentless drive towards mechanisation and modernity, however, had its own industrial casualties – not just people – and some of them were quite unexpected, a notable example being the lot of the miller.

The neat and tidy image presented by the casting house in the foundry at the National Slate Museum in Dinorwig in North Wales, *opposite page*, contrasts vividly with the actual working conditions illustrated in the postcard c.1908, *below left*, of steel casting at the British Westinghouse Company's factory in Manchester's Trafford Park.

below: Hereford Waterworks' beam engine was built by Harvey of Hayle in 1851. Now driven by electricity, it is seen here in motion during an open day.

right: Wilton Windmill today, beautifully restored after having been abandoned in 1914. Restoration started in 1976. The mill not only has cast-iron machinery rather than wood, it also has a heavy cast-iron cap. During restoration, that was erected using a large crane. Just how it was raised into position in 1821 remains unclear.

below left: The cast-iron drive gearing — known as the 'wallower' inside the cap of the windmill. These gears convert the rotative motion from the sails into the horizontal rotation needed to rotate the millstone.

below right: Wilton's cast-iron cap and drive shaft.

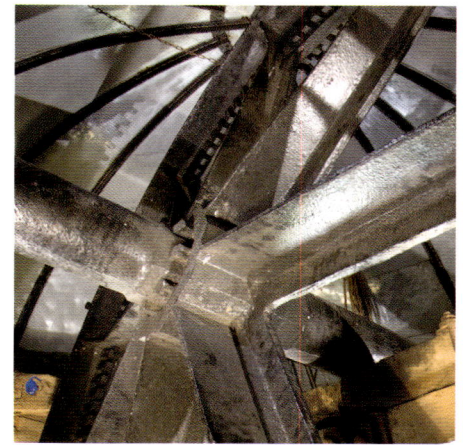

INTRODUCTION

Across many parts of Britain in the late eighteenth century, the windmill was already quite rare. The watermill had become the dominant method of milling flour – wind speed was variable, while through lades and sluices, the water supply's flow rate could be controlled and relied on, thereby increasing the number of days on which the mill was operational. At harvest-time such reliability was a bonus.

Industrial progress can often lead to unexpected consequences, and during the canal building era, the demand for water to keep locks working meant that at least some of the flow of rivers was diverted. The building of the Kennet & Avon Canal in Wiltshire needed a steam-powered pumping station – at Crofton – to raise water to its highest levels, and providing that water from the local River Bedwyn effectively put watermills on the river out of business.

So Wilton Windmill, just a few miles from Crofton, had to be built to take the place of the watermills. Windmills may already have been 'old technology' by 1821 when it was built, but Wilton was considered to be 'state of the art', built with cast iron rather than wooden machinery. It served the local community until the outbreak of the Great War.

The Kennet and Avon Canal, on the other hand, never fulfilled it potential – the long distance canal traffic from Bristol to London predicted in the canal company's business plans just never materialised. However, both the canal and the windmill survive as popular tourist attractions.

below left: Although of about the same age, Bursledon Windmill in Hampshire is of a quite different design. The cap – known as the 'boat' – is wooden, and there is no fantail to point the sails towards the wind. The cap has to be rotated by the miller or his assistant using the wheel and chain mechanism at the back of the cap.

below right: Inside Bursledon mill, the machinery is wooden, of a design which had been used for over a century. Travelling millwrights were kept busy replacing wooden teeth broken off by sudden changes in wind-speed. Most of the machinery was replaced when the mill was restored in the 1990s.

24

ABOUT TIME

OUR OBSESSION WITH TIME is a relatively recent thing, a result of – or at least encouraged by – our ability to measure it down to unimaginably small fractions of a second. In the qualifying session for a Formula 1 Grand Prix a few years ago, one driver was described as being "off the pace by a massive seven-tenths of a second", making that sound as if he was really slow. Yet we could barely even snap our fingers in seven-tenths of a second.

Knowing the time only really became important when the craftsman moved from being a self-employed home-worker to being an employee in a factory, and had to make the change from working only when there was sufficient daylight, to working fixed hours under artificial lighting.

Wherever one worked, until 1840, measuring time had essentially been a local matter, based simply on the position of the sun. Thus noon in London was separated by several minutes from noon in Plymouth or Truro.

opposite: The second oldest working clock in the world – in Wells Cathedral in Somerset – dates from c.1390. The gold 'sun' marks the hour, the gold star the minutes.

below: Salisbury Cathedral's late-fourteenth-century clock is claimed to be the oldest working clock in the world. The original wrought iron mechanism is in remarkable condition for its age, having largely been constructed around 1386.

above: For mill and factory workers, the time-clock was part of everyday working life. The one is from Dundee's Verdant Jute Works.

above right: The time clock from Bowler's mineral water factory in Bath – now displayed in the Museum of Bath at Work – was built by the National Time Recorder Company in Kent.

Factory work brought with it a whole range of changes in everyday life. It introduced the need to 'clock on' and 'clock off' at work; it introduced the idea of the hooter which was sounded to let the workforce know it was time to get to work – quickly – and the hooter, again, to mark the end of the working shift. And as the machinery in most factories was steam-powered, the hooter or whistle was driven by the same steam engine which drove the looms, lathes and other tools.

The need for punctuality also introduced the role of the 'knocker-upper' who, for a small weekly fee, would rattle a long pole on front bedroom windows to make sure you didn't oversleep – and thus clock on late and earn a reprimand or even a fine.

The 'occupation' was of sufficient importance and novelty for Leo H. Grindon to mention it in his 1882 *History of Lancashire*.

'In Manchester there are professional "knockers-up" – men whose business it is to tap at up-stair windows with a long wand, when the time comes to arouse the sleeper from his pillow.'

In the 1880s, the going rate for a 'knocker-up' in Manchester was usually around a shilling a week, but rates varied across the country and some people got paid much more.

Whatever the cost, it was obviously cheaper than risking losing wages, or even losing one's job after persistent lateness.

One woman, a Mrs Waters from Yorkshire, who had made a substantial income out of the job, told the Canadian *Huron Expositor* newspaper of her experiences in an article 'Experiences of a Knocker-up' on 22 March 1878. She was more than happy to discuss the source of her income.

It had started after her husband was injured in an accident in the foundry in which he worked, and Mrs Waters had gone to collect the small pension he had been granted.

> 'I got into conversation with one of the better sort of men who were employed in the works [and told him] that I was willing to do anything that would help [pay the bills] when he said, quite suddenly like, "If you will knock me up at 3 o'clock every morning but Sunday, I will give you half-a-crown a week."... The reason that knocking-up is so widespread nowadays is this: people get so used to the alarum-clock that it fails to awake them, or if it awake them, they are, at times, so sleepy that they drop off again before the alarum runs out.'

The skill of the 'knocker-up' or 'knocker-upper' was to waken only those who were paying him, and not the neighbours on either side. He also had to move around his area quickly if a number of his customers' factory shifts all started at the same time. This image, which is thought to be from either North Lancashire or Yorkshire, comes from a postcard produced in the early 1900s.

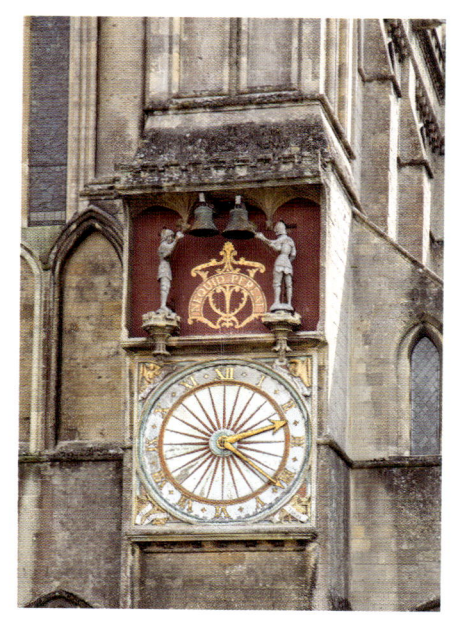

Within a year, she had more than thirty customers on her round but not, she was quick to point out, all at such a high weekly rate – she charged much less to those needing to be wakened up at 5am or 6am.

Given that wages were not particularly generous, paying a knocker-up having already invested in an 'alarum clock' might seem an extravagance.

Since mediaeval times, the majority of clocks had been found inside churches and abbeys, their bells used to call the faithful to the many services which were held each day, and several spectacular 'astronomical clocks' can still be seen in the great mediaeval cathedrals.

Putting clock faces on church towers is a much later innovation – usually dating from the second half of the nineteenth century – and on many such towers, it is quite obvious that the towers were not originally intended to have clocks on them.

As churches and town halls were the most prominent buildings in most towns, they were the first to be fitted with highly visible 'public' clocks.

The oldest working clock in the world is said to be the one in Salisbury Cathedral, which has been dated to around 1386 – although there are earlier (and unsupported) claims from churches in France and Spain – while the astronomical clock which still attracts crowds at Wells Cathedral in Somerset dates from just four years later in 1390.

ABOUT TIME

The Salisbury clock was originally located in a freestanding bell tower, to the north of the cathedral nave which was demolished in the late 1700s. The site was excavated a few years ago – appropriately by tv's *Time Team*.

The clock has no face and its purpose was simply to ring the bells in advance of each of the cathedral's many daily services. Drive came from two large stone weights, and it had to be re-wound every few days.

Taken out of service long ago, stored in the cathedral's tower and largely forgotten about until re-discovered in the 1920s, it was restored in 1956, and moved to its present position in the north nave aisle.

The Wells clock – which actually has two faces, one inside, one outside – strikes every fifteen minutes when jousting knights on horseback charge at each other on the interior face.

Ralph Erghum, Bishop of Salisbury until 1388, is believed to have commissioned the Salisbury clock, and as he later became Bishop of Bath and Wells, it has been suggested he may also have commissioned that clock as well.

Until 2010, the clock was still wound by hand – an onerous task – but with the retirement of the last 'Keeper of the Great Clock of Wells', it has been driven by an electric motor, at which time the original mechanism was moved to London's Science Museum where it is still manually wound and can be seen doing what it was designed to do.

below: J. B. Joyce's 1931 mechanical clock displayed at St Laurence's church in Ludlow, Shropshire.

opposite top: The exterior face of the Wells Cathedral clock probably dates from the early years of the fifteenth century, although it was driven by the same mechanism as the earlier interior face.

opposite bottom: Exeter Cathedral's astronomical clock is said to date from 1484. In 1885, Gillett & Bland of Croydon replaced the fifteenth century mechanism.

right: The carillon at St Laurence's church Ludlow, played a different tune each day of the week. On Sunday it was Psalm 104, Monday 'See the Conquering Hero', Tuesday 'Bluebells of Scotland', Wednesday Psalm 113, Thursday 'My Lodging is on Cold Ground', Friday 'Life let us Cherish' and Saturday 'Home Sweet Home'. The tunes were played at 8am, 12 noon and 8pm after the hour had been struck.

opposite top: Northiam Station's 1900 clock is now preserved in the Colonel Stephens Museum at Tenterden Station on the Kent & East Sussex Railway.

middle: A humorous Edwardian postcard published by Bamforth & Company of Holmfirth, Yorkshire.

bottom: Sheringham Station's clock on the North Norfolk Railway. The station is now the terminus of the heritage line.

The clock has two dials – the ornate astronomical face inside the cathedral, and the much simpler but later one which faces out from the north transept.

In the south aisle of St Laurence's church in Ludlow, the last of the many mechanical clocks which served the community over the years can be seen. It was built in 1931 by J. B. Joyce & Company of Whitchurch in Shropshire, who had started building long-case clocks two hundred and forty years earlier in 1691.

There are many other examples of clocks by Joyce including the Diamond Jubilee Clock from 1897 over Eastgate Street in Chester, and the station clocks at Liverpool Lime Street, at Aberystwyth, and at Carnforth in Lancashire.

Also preserved in Ludlow church – this time in the north aisle – is the former 'carillon' – the wrought iron mechanism with projecting pins which drove the peal of bells. Powered by the clock itself, the carillon is like a giant musical box, its metal pins playing a different tune – at 8am, noon and 8pm

– for each day of the week. While the mechanism largely dates from 1890, the selection of tunes originated in 1795.

For the wealthier members of society, the need to know the time introduced the idea of carrying a pocket watch – an expensive and treasured item which was protected from loss or theft by being attached by a chain to its owner.

Surprisingly, portable timepieces date back to the sixteenth century and the innovation of using an integral spring instead of an external weight to provide the drive, initially in clocks, but quickly followed by watches.

The first ones were produced in Germany, followed by Italy, with British watch and clockmakers making their first portable timepieces just a few years later.

Some names, of course, are well known – John Harrison the Yorkshire-born, Lincolnshire-based carpenter who taught himself clockmaking in the early eighteenth century is probably the most famous – his early clocks and marine chronometers were capable of hitherto unheard-of accuracy – said to be within one second a month.

The movements in his earliest long-case clocks were made of wood, and his innovative designs for the mechanisms produced clocks which required relatively little maintenance and yet provided accuracy which had never been possible before.

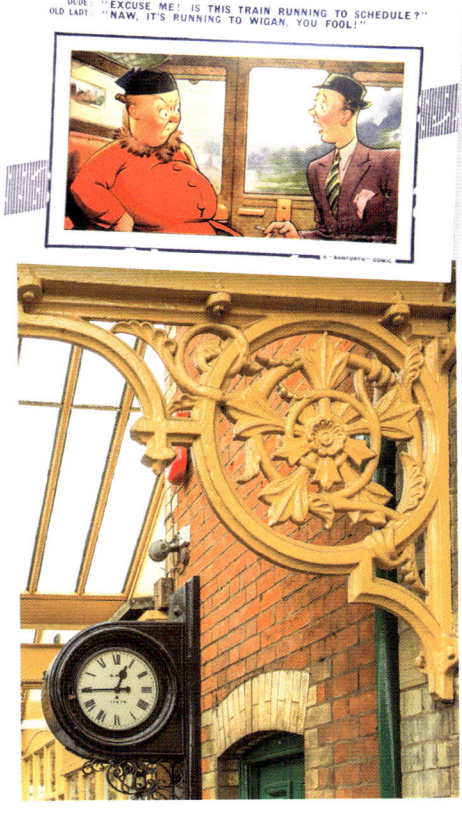

above: The station clock at Carnforth, from an Edwardian postcard. Railway clocks proliferated in the second half of the nineteenth century, and ensuring they kept precise time was one of the many responsibilities of the Station Master.

middle: Clocking off at the huge Singer sewing machine factory in Clydebank seems to have been 3pm, if the clock on the factory tower is to be believed. Many of these workers are making their way to the suburban railway station.

right: Dinner time at the Huntley & Palmer biscuit factory in Reading c.1904. Factory life brought with it strict adherence to time-keeping, and regulated hours for such things as start and finish times, and meal breaks.

left: When the Liverpool & Manchester Railway's No.57 Lion entered service in 1837 'local time' in the two cities was separated by around three minutes. It is seen here, in steam, during the recreation of the famous Rainhill Trials in 1980. Lion – which starred in the 1953 Ealing comedy *The Titfield Thunderbolt* – is now on static display in the Museum of Liverpool.

below: A Great Western Railway clock in Claverton Pumping Station – built in 1808 by John Rennie – which raised water from the River Avon 48 feet up to the Kennet & Avon Canal. The GWR whose main line runs alongside the station had owned the canal since 1852.

Examples of these revolutionary timepieces can be seen in the Royal Observatory at Greenwich, the Science Museum, and Leeds City Museum.

Harrison is best known for the application of his ideas to marine chronometers and his work in establishing a means of accurately identifying longitude – in other words, being able to work out exactly where a ship was when it was out of sight of land.

Back on land, it was not until the arrival of the railway that 'keeping time' became an important issue, and the Great Western Railway was the first to introduce 'standard' or 'railway time' across its network in 1840 – based on London time, of course.

There was a great deal of resistance to the idea, and it was not immediately or widely accepted, and for a few years, while the GWR used its 'standard' time, the towns and cities along the route still adhered to local time, resisting attempts to make them adopt what they thought of as the imposition of 'London time'.

above: A bold statement of civic wealth – Bolton Town Hall was designed by Leeds architect William Hill and opened by the Prince of Wales in 1873. The clock on its lofty tower is visible right across town.

above right: The clock on Bristol's Corn Exchange, displaying both 'Bristol time' and 'London time'. The Grade I listed building was designed and built between 1741 and 1743 by John Wood the Elder. The clock, however, was not inserted into the facade until 1822. Bristol only adopted Standard Time in 1852, five years after most of the country had done so.

To get round the difference some places even used clocks which had two minute hands, one showing local time, the other 'railway time'. A notable example still survives on Bristol's Corn Exchange with the clock showing 'London time' on the red minute hand and 'Bristol time' on the black one, separated by eleven minutes.

In 1847 broad agreement was reached that 'Standard Time' – which would become known as 'Greenwich Mean Time' – would be adopted nationally by all the many railway companies.

The London & North Western Railway adopted it in 1847, with the Caledonian Railway and most other companies doing so the following year.

Perhaps surprisingly, the first of George Bradshaw's famous railway timetables was published in 1839, several years before the widespread adoption of 'standard time', so the printed arrival and departure times at each station were in local time – potentially confusing for through-passengers making journey times appear to be a few minutes shorter when travelling west than they did when travelling east.

Back then, of course, there were still relatively few railways, so that first edition of *Bradshaw's Railway Companion Containing the Times of Departure, Fares &c. of the Railways of England* ran to only eight pages. By the early years of the twentieth century, it would run to well over a thousand.

One the its more surprising inclusions in early editions was the note that on the London & South Western Railway's services from Vauxhall, London, to Southampton, 'Third Class Passengers will be taken by the Goods Trains'.

Although 'standard time', 'railway time' or 'Greenwich Mean Time', was widely used across the country after the railways adopted it, and already widely used as a reference time by mariners worldwide, it was not actually enshrined in British law until 2 August 1880.

The General Election, which had been held earlier that year, was the last one where Polling Stations across the country were opened and closed using 'local time'.

It is quite remarkable that such monumental changes in how time finally became standardised happened only a hundred and forty years ago.

We have travelled a long way to a situation where absolute precision as far as time is concerned is what keeps the world and all its machines ticking. Without that precision, every one of the electronic devices we use in our everyday lives would cease to work reliably.

There are anomalies. The 'pips' before the news on Radio 4 – and by which people used to set their watches – are several seconds later on digital radios than on analogue ones. But which one of them is accurate? Actually it's analogue.

below: The 1880 General Election which was fought between the Conservatives under Disraeli and the Liberals under Gladstone, was held just before a standard nationwide time was introduced.

below left: An electric clock advertising the use of electricity at the Amberley Museum & Heritage Centre.

35

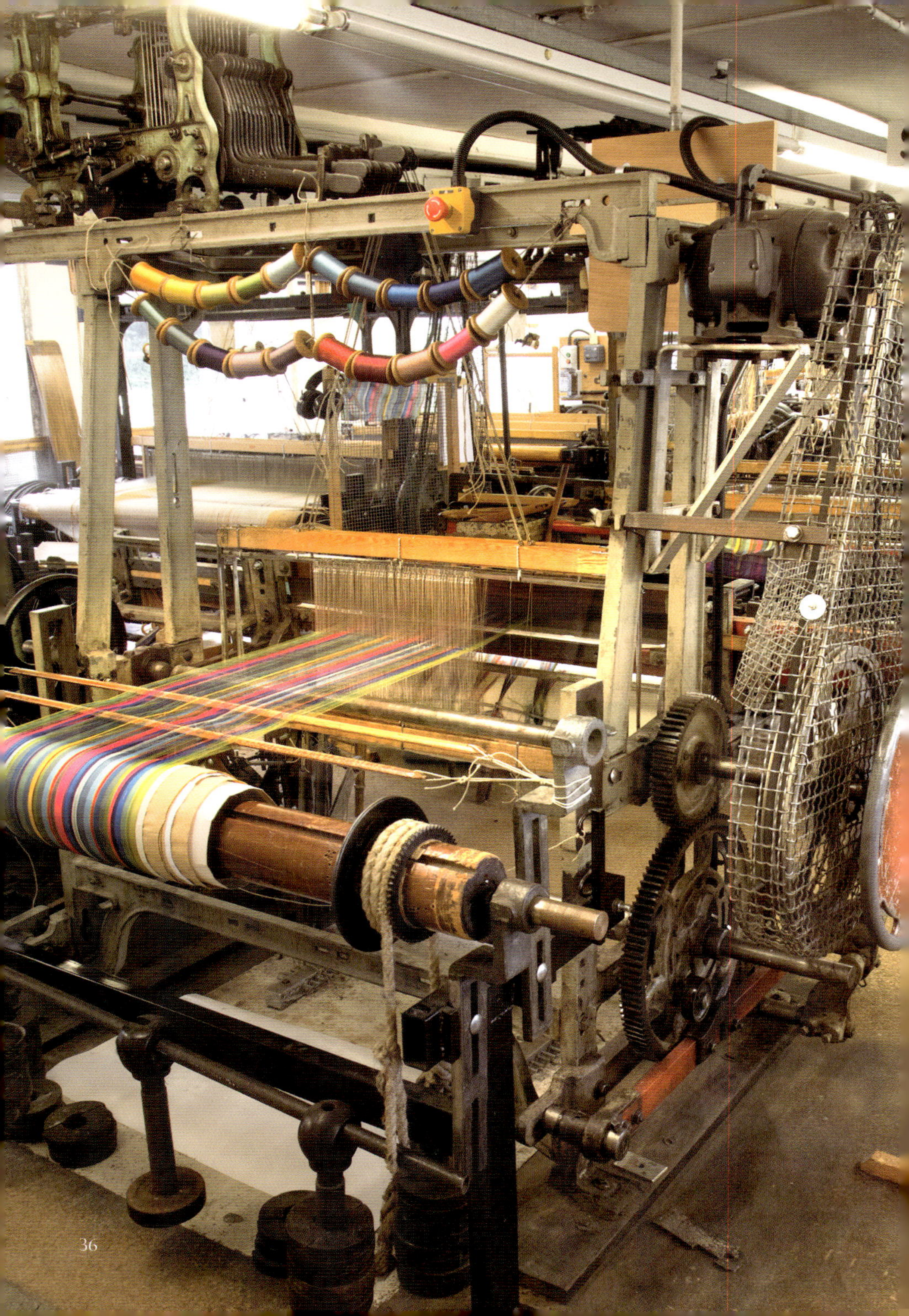

THE RISE AND DEMISE OF THE MILL

NOT ALL MILLS WERE DARK AND SATANIC – despite Blake's often-used soubriquet and, initially, not all mills were large. While the great nineteenth century textile mills which dominated places such as Wigan, Bolton, Galashiels, Selkirk and elsewhere are well known, many smaller rural mills were established wherever there was locally-produced wool to be processed. At a time when there were poor roads and a limited transport infrastructure, local mills made sense.

The relentless growth of large industrial mills in towns and cities may have driven most of them out of business, but a rare few survive.

Whitchurch Silk Mill in Hampshire started out as a fulling mill in 1800, being re-equipped as a silk weaving mill by 1817. By 1846, its workforce had grown to more than a hundred people – 40% of whom were children under the age of thirteen.

opposite page: Whitchurch Silk Mill in Hampshire was originally built as a fulling mill in 1800 and converted to silk-making by William Madick in 1817.

below: A brightly-coloured warp on one of Whitchurch Mill's silk looms.

38

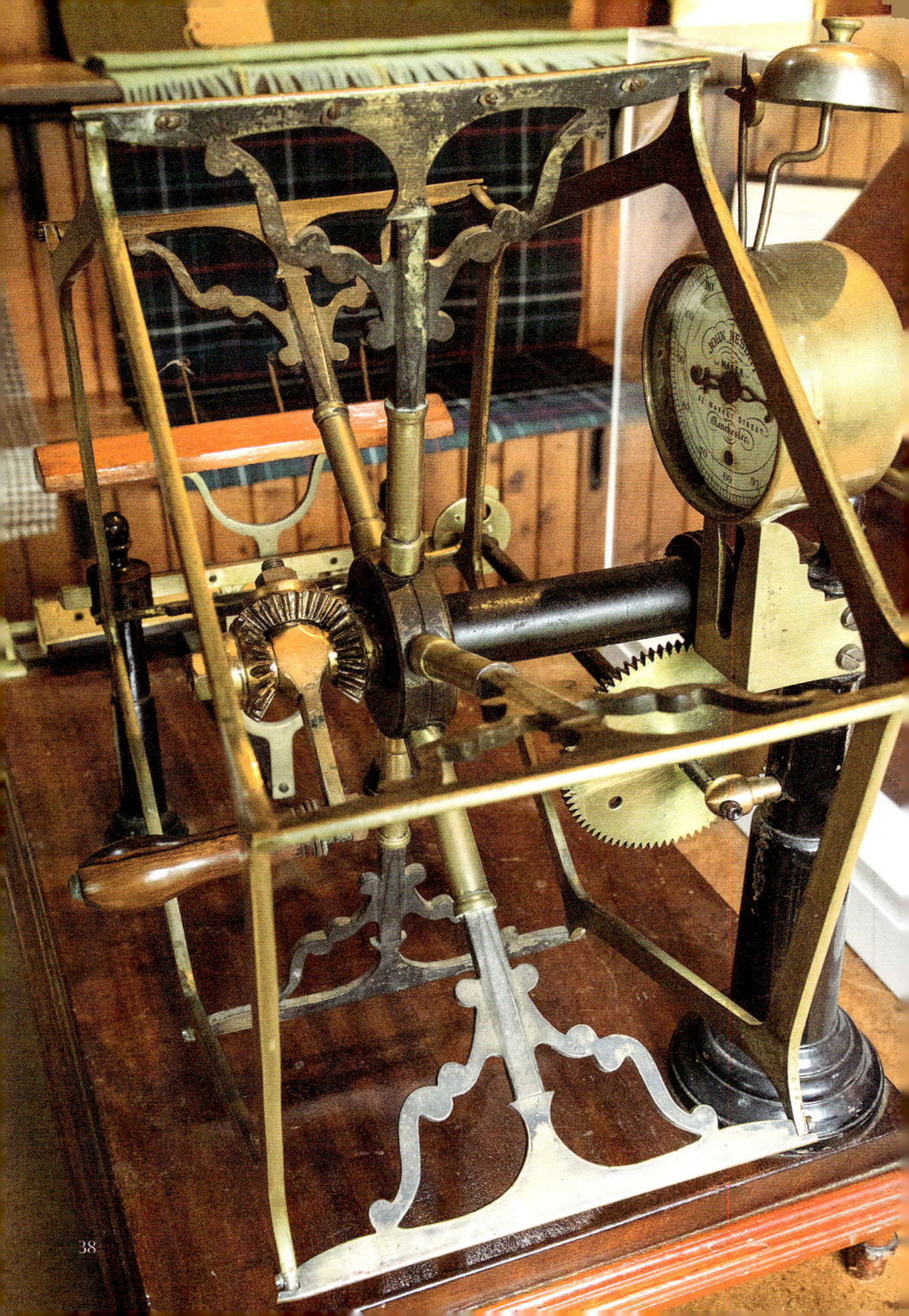

THE RISE AND DEMISE OF THE MILL

Now restored and open to the public, the mill's eighteen looms range in date from the 1890s to the 1960s. Originally powered by the mill's large water-wheel, they are driven by electricity today.

Another small water-powered mill – the Knockando Woolmill in the Spey Valley near Aberlour in Moray – is a 'Category A' listed industrial site – that's the same as Grade I listing south of the border – so it's pretty special. In Gaelic, its name is Cnoc-an-Dhu, meaning 'little black hill'.

Beautifully restored, and with the addition of a new commercial weaving shed and educational area, Knockando Mill is well worth a visit as it epitomises the hundreds of small mills which were once a common sight throughout the country.

The mill was first mentioned in 1784 when it was described as a 'Waukmill' – the word 'wauking' described the process of fulling woollen cloth by pounding it against a board or large flat stone, and stretching it with the hands and feet, but was later applied to a mechanised version of the same process. By the

opposite page: A Victorian Hank-winder made by John Nesbitt of Manchester, used to check the quality and weight of a pre-set length of wool. This one is displayed in the mill shop at Knockando Woolmill in Speyside.

left: In Edwardian times, there was even a market for postcards of factory buildings. This is Samuel Courtauld's Townsford Mill in Halstead c.1904. The building still survives today.

below: Detail of the wooden mill wheel at Whitchurch Silk Mill in Hampshire.

39

right: The little water-powered mill building at Knockando is a far cry from the typical large mill complex in which most of Britain's textiles were manufactured.

middle: By the early years of the twentieth century, handloom weaving had been restricted to no more than a craft industry in most areas, its nostalgia value celebrated in postcards. Luxury fabrics such as Harris Tweed were still woven on hand looms by home weavers, and even today, the lone weaver working at home is still an essential feature of Harris Tweed's unique character. Today, craft weaving is growing in popularity as more and more people look for distinctiveness in the fabrics with which they dress themselves or decorate their homes.

below: Girls demonstrating 'wauking' or 'walking' the tweed at the Imperial International Exhibition in London's White City in 1909 — one of a series of postcards purporting to show traditional Scottish crafts, published by Valentine of Dundee.

THE RISE AND DEMISE OF THE MILL

Victorian era, the term had strangely been corrupted in some tweed-making areas to 'walking'. After cloth had been 'wauked' it was stretched on to 'tenter-hooks' and air-dried either outdoors or in drying sheds.

The mill could also have been used for the washing, dyeing and carding of raw wool, but as there was a carding mill about half a mile away, that was probably not the case in its earliest days.

All that changed in 1829 when a nearby carding mill was destroyed by flooding – an event which may have directly led to the expansion of Knockando's activities. Certainly wool dyeing was carried out there by 1841 when the tenant-farmers, Janet and James Grant were listed in the Census returns as 'wool dyers'.

below: The spinning mules in Knockando Woolmill, Speyside, were made by Platts of Oldham in 1870.

bottom left: The Knockando Teasel Gig used natural teasels to raise the nap on blankets. Being a natural product, the teasels very quickly lost their spikes, and replacing them was a regular and time-consuming task.

bottom right: Teasels – botanic name *Dipsacus fullonum* and also known as the 'common teasel' or 'fuller's teasel' – on display in the Knockando Mill shop. Later napping gigs used metal teeth to raise the nap on blankets, but to many woollen mill owners, nothing worked quite as well, or as gently, as the natural teasel. If a teasel came across an irregularity in the cloth, it would break. If a metal tooth came across the same, it could tear the cloth. In the nineteenth century, the teasels used in most blanket mills would have been grown locally, some of the plants growing to more than 2.0 metres tall. They were harvested in the autumn and dried for use the following year.

below: Knockando's Hutchinson & Hollingsworth Dobcross looms date from 1896 and 1899 respectively and were built at the company's Atlas Works on Colne Road in the Diggle area of Huddersfield. Founded in 1860, Hutchinson & Hollingsworth became a major manufacturer of power looms — originally belt or chain-driven — especially Dobcross machines. They closed down in 1967. The Dobcross loom, also known as the 'Dobby' loom, allows different warp threads to be separately lifted or lowered to enable small to medium area designs to be woven into the fabric, such as with tartans. It is a much simpler loom than the Jacquard, but the principle is similar. It is equipped with a drop-box motion which contains shuttles of weft with different colours which can be positioned immediately before each particular coloured yarn is required for insertion. The loom uses the so-called underpick weft system where the warp is pulled down to allow shuttle travel rather than being lifted upwards.

A small rural, or community, mills such as Knockando would have originally been set up to serve the immediate farming community at a time when transport was poor in the Highlands, and the handloom weaver still held sway.

Initially, it might only have worked seasonally when the sheep had been sheared and there were fleeces to process. In busier times in the farming community, the Grants would have worked on their land themselves. The output of mills like this was woven into tweeds and blankets.

Spinning in the eighteenth century was usually carried out by women working with individual spinning wheels but that changed when the semi-mechanised water-powered 'spinning jenny' was introduced. That could spin eight or sixteen threads at a time – a huge improvement on Granny working alone at her spinning-wheel, but still very limited. The spinning mule changed all that.

Knockando did not get its first fully mechanised self-acting spinning mule until 1870, and is one of the few pieces of equipment on site today which was bought new.

The other machinery was all bought second-hand from larger neighbouring mills when they were upgrading their facilities. The most modern piece of machinery still operational in the restored sheds at Knockando is

THE RISE AND DEMISE OF THE MILL

left: Don Mill in Middleton near Manchester was typical of hundreds of large mills built across the north of England in the last quarter of the nineteenth century. It was opened in 1899.

below: Inside the weaving shed in an Edwardian cotton mill in Walton-de-Dale, Lancashire. The daily inhalation of cotton dust in the damp atmosphere of the mill played havoc with the health of the workforce — mainly young girls — leading to tuberculosis and early death for many. A popular saying was 'Britain's bread hangs on Lancashire's thread'.

approaching 100 years old. All the modern equipment is in an adjacent new shed.

The mule came from Platt Brothers & Company of Oldham, Lancashire – a company more used to supplying much larger mules to the giant mills of Lancashire and Yorkshire than to a district mill in rural Scotland.

The single 120-thread machine would have initiated a major increase in the mill's output, but must have been an

43

above left & right: The spinning mules at Coldharbour Mill in Devon.

right: Hall I'th Wood in Bolton was home to Samuel Crompton in the late eighteenth century. His invention of the 'Spinning Jenny' was hugely important in introducing mechanisation to the textile industry.

unusually small order for Platt Brothers who were already the world's largest manufacturer of textile machinery, employing more than 7000 people at their Werneth factory in Oldham.

The new mule was belt-driven from the mill's modestly-sized water-wheel fed from the Knockando Burn. To keep the mule supplied with carded wool, a much larger carding machine was installed,

THE RISE AND DEMISE OF THE MILL

Carding was the technique used to blend and straighten the woollen fibres and to even them out, thus ensuring an even thickness in the 'slub' – a loose rope of fibres. The carder at Knockando is fitted with a 'Scotch Feed' which

OLD SPINNING JENNY.

left: Crompton's Spinning Jenny, published as a postcard c.1910 by Richard Howarth & Co., 'Cotton Spinners, Manufacturers & Doublers' of Tatton Mills, Ordsall, Manchester.

below: Locally produced postcards c.1910 give a flavour of the cramped working conditions. Some — as at bottom left — contained cautionary messages about quality control. Both these cards were produced for a cotton mill in Nelson, Lancashire.

45

above: Children as young as twelve learning to operate Jacquard power looms at Kershaw's Derby Street Cotton Mill in Bolton c.1920.

below: The Apprentice House at Samuel Greg's Styal Mill in Cheshire, where children were used as a cheap source of labour. Ninety children — some as young as eight years old — lived in the Apprentice House in the eighteenth century, where they were probably given a better lifestyle than they would have endured in the workhouse. In exchange for food, clothes and board, they were trained for a life in the mill.

further blended and mixed the fibres, ensuring more even colour as well as further smoothing the slub. To achieve this the 'Scotch Feed' took the carded slubbings, turned them by 90 degrees and fed them back on to the carder.

The slubs were then fed into a reducer or condenser creating the soft lengths of wool which could then be drawn, twisted and spun on the mules. Everything else is a matter of scale – the machinery found at Knockando is exactly the same as would have been found in larger mills. The only difference is scale – while Knockando had a single 120-thread spinning mule, for example, a large cotton mill would have had a building full of them. Once ring spinning started to replace mules, the numbers increased dramatically.

At Wigan's huge Trencherfield cotton mill, the mules could spin 24,000 threads at a time, while the ring spinning frames increased that total to more than 84,000, but that was relatively small by comparison with Atlas Mills in Bolton, however, which in its heyday had 400,000 spindles, making it one of the most extensive cotton spinning facilities in the country. One of the former stores there is now home to the Northern Mill Engine Society's Bolton Steam Museum where a large collection of industrial steam engines – rescued from mills and industrial facilities across the region – has been assembled, with many having been restored to working order.

The museum organises regular 'steaming days' throughout the year.

Ring spinning had many advantages over mules – the machinery took up less space, was safer, faster, less prone to thread breakages, and therefore more profitable.

A ring spinning shed could also be operated by considerably fewer workers than a mule room – a very powerful incentive for owners intent on both modernisation and cost cutting – which of course meant maximising profits.

In the early years of the nineteenth century, even towns like Wigan – which would become one of the country's leading producers of cotton – still relied heavily on the employment of large numbers of hand-loom weavers working in the lofts on the upper floors of their houses.

above: An early treddle-operated hand loom displayed in Dundee's Verdant Jute Works.

left: A hand-loom weaver at work on his treddle loom, from a series of promotional postcards produced c.1908 by Richard Howarth & Co. Ltd, Cotton Spinners, Manufacturers & Doublers of Tatton Mills, Ordsall, Manchester. The cards were printed in Berlin.

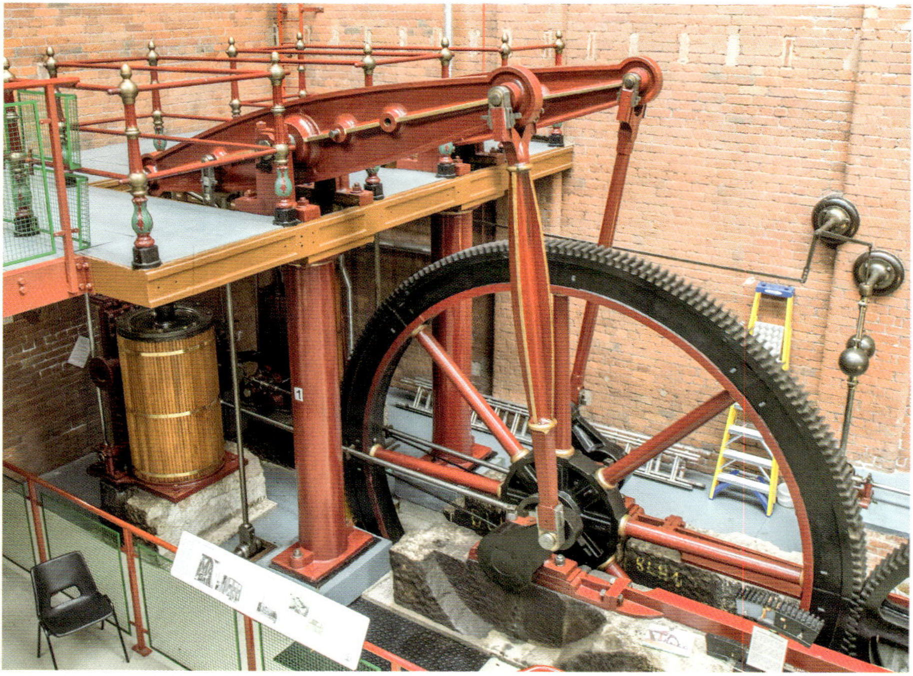

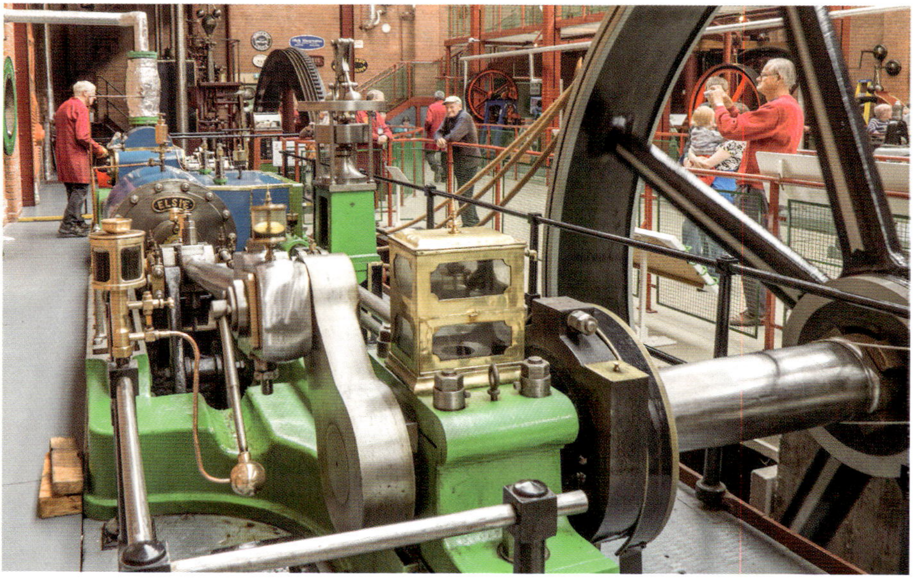
ELSIE

THE RISE AND DEMISE OF THE MILL

While large spinning mills were becoming a feature of the town's skyline, more than 2000 weavers under contract to just one company – John Rylands – still worked in their own home lofts. Rylands was just one of the town's many cotton mills, so the number of weavers still working their hand looms at home would have been very much larger.

However, as demand for cotton grew, the home weaver represented a considerable bottleneck in the supply chain. The water-driven power loom, introduced in the 1780s, would eventually sound the death-knell of cotton weaving on hand looms, and would itself soon be replaced by steam.

By 1835, the eleven large mechanised mills then working in the town had nearly 5000 men, women and children working in them. For a town with a population of just 11,000, that was hugely significant.

By the mid 1860s the number of mill workers had grown to 9000, but with Wigan heavily dependent upon imported American cotton – supplies of which had all but ceased

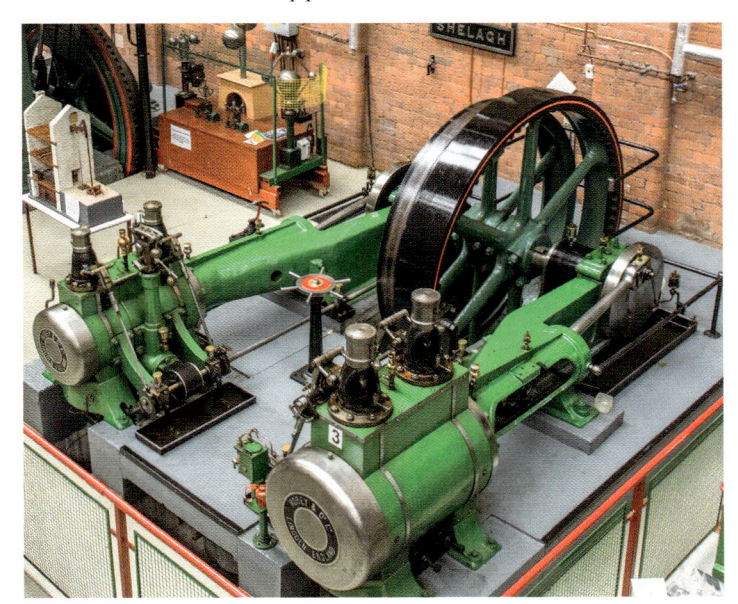

above: The author, under instruction, having been invited to start Bolton Steam Museum's 1915-built inverted vertical compound engine from the Diamond Ropeworks at Royton.

below: The 1935 Robey cross-compound engine was used to teach students about steam engineering at the Manchester College of Science & Technology.

opposite top: Built in 1840, this double beam engine worked at Crossfield Mill in Rochdale until decommissioned in 1953. It is the oldest engine in the Bolton Steam Museum collection.

opposite bottom: 'Elsie', a 180hp engine, was built in 1902 for the Barchant Spinning Company, by J. & W. McNaught of Rochdale. It is also now in Bolton Steam Museum.

49

right & below: A volunteer at work on one of the silk handlooms at Cartwright & Sheldon's Paradise Silk Mill in Macclesfield, Cheshire. A keen eye is needed to repair breaks in the silk warp — there can be several thousand individual threads to be threaded through the loom's harness and if one breaks, finding it and tying it can be tricky.

during the Civil War — 7000 of them were out of work.

The shift from home industry to industrial-scale production was most rapid in the manufacture of cotton, leading to the construction of literally hundreds of large mills, the majority of them in Lancashire nd Yorkshire.

As textile mills got larger, the power needed to operate them grew enormously — in turn leading to the development and construction of the largest — and finest — Victorian and Edwardian steam engines ever built. But for the dedication of small groups of enthusiasts, they would almost certainly all have been lost when the steam age came to an end.

Significant amongst those groups has been the Northern Mill Engine Society which, over more than fifty years, has saved a large collection of important engines from destruction.

The fruits of their labours can be enjoyed in the remarkable Bolton Steam Museum housed in the former cotton store of Bolton's Atlas No.3 Mill — part of what was once one of the largest mill complexes in the country — where

THE RISE AND DEMISE OF THE MILL

their large collection of textile mill engines can be enjoyed – and occasionally seen working under steam power.

With finer fabrics, that transition was in many cases much more gradual, and delicate silks continued to be woven on manual looms long after the production of cotton and wool products had become mechanised – early machinery was just not gentle enough on fine yarns.

In several cases, mechanisation simply never happened. Hand-loom weaving of silks is a classic example, with the likes of Macclesfield's Paradise Mill using manually operated treddle looms for its entire productive life.

A visit to Paradise Mill today is a real step back in time. The only difference is that the noise and bustle has gone, the rows of ancient looms standing quiet as if the weavers have stepped out to lunch.

The guided tour encompasses every stage of the production process, from the raw silk cocoons to the finished fabrics, expertly explained along the way with demonstrations of weaving on the mill's Jacquard hand-looms, some of which were already more than 120 years old when they ceased to be used commercially in 1981.

below: When this picture was taken inside the Dorma weaving shed in Wigan in 1987, it was the last working weaving shed in the town. It closed shortly afterwards. The weaving shed was equipped with Belgian Picanol looms – much faster than the company's previous American-built Northrop looms – and manufactured cotton bedding. When the Picanol looms were initially installed, one weaver became responsible for 30 looms, rather than 20 which had been the norm with the Northrops in the 1950s. By 1987, however, the shed's 180 looms were worked in shifts by just 10 weavers. A century earlier, with hand looms, it had been one weaver to one loom – that century had seen a huge reduction in the necessary manpower.

right: Generations of people spent their entire lives in the same two-up-two-down terraced houses which lined the streets around the large mills, summoned to work each day by the insistent shrill of the mill whistle. The spinning and weaving companies were the towns' major employers and, in many cases, also the landlords of those who tenanted the houses. After the mills closed in the 1950s, '60s and '70s, the vast buildings were sometimes left for decades to become derelict eyesores, while many of the houses were offered for sale to their tenants.

below right: Coldharbour Mill's two-cylinder horizontal cross-compound engine generating nearly 300hp was built by Pollit & Wigzell of Sowerby Bridge in Yorkshire. It was installed new in 1910, replacing two earlier beam engines, and powered the mill until 1981. Today, much of the machinery is driven by a huge 5.4 metre diameter water wheel — water had been the mill's original power source when it opened in 1799.

THE RISE AND DEMISE OF THE MILL

Ninety years ago, Macclesfield still had 250 hand-loom silk weavers, now there are none.

The silk mills which are still in production in Britain today were mechanised – first by water power and later by electricity – almost a century before operations ceased at Paradise. The scale of silk weaving in Victorian Macclesfield was immense – more than seventy mills were operating in the mid-nineteenth century, and Paradise now stands alone as a testament to the town's hand-loom weavers.

So large was that workforce that a Sunday School was built in 1814 to cater for up to 2000 mill workers' children. It had to be a Sunday School, of course, as during the rest of the week most of the children would themselves have been employed in the mills.

The introduction of steam power elsewhere in the industry, a gradual process from the 1820s, also heralded the introduction of a range of entirely new skills into the industry – engineers. Whether it be controlling the engine itself, or maintaining the increasingly complex spinning and weaving machinery, engineers became key figures in keeping the mills running smoothly and efficiently.

below: A hand-tinted late Victorian glass magic lantern slide showing an engineer adjusting the spinning mules in an unknown mill. This image comes from a series of industrial slides produced in the 1890s. Some of these series were designed as instructional and training aids, but most were used as illustrations for public lectures in village halls. As few members of the general public away from the big centres of the textile industry ever saw the inside of a mill, or knew what went on there, such evening talks were usually well attended.

54

THE RISE AND DEMISE OF THE MILL

The nineteenth century was, of course, a time of great advances in technology, and to meet the growing demand for a skilled workforce, colleges opened up across the country training these new key figures. Engineering in its many forms became essential to Victorian development.

Over the following century, labour laws and working conditions would slowly be improved, but for most of the nineteenth century, the nation's workforce would be increasingly drawn into the large towns and cities, to work in ever larger mills and factories as the age of the home craftsman ended.

The relentless growth of the large cotton mill, however, was over by the Great War, and for the next fifty years or

left: A postcard c.1905 of the Warping Room at John Rylands' Gidlow Mill in Wigan — hundreds of wooden bobbins as far as the eye can see.

below: Setting up a warp at Coldharbour Mill in Devon, the yarns wound on cardboard cores rather than wooden bobbins.

opposite page: Also at Coldharbour Mill, thousands of redundant bobbin.

right: The woodyard at Stott Park Bobbin Mill in Cumbria, a good supply of coppiced timber stacked and ready for future use. The site is now in the care of English Heritage and open to visitors daily.

so, those Victorian mills continued to produce cotton in vast quantities.

But lack of investment in new equipment – and the short-sighted post-war policy of selling off machinery to emerging economies such as India – proved the industry's downfall.

Mill owners should have seen that coming, but sadly didn't. They just continued banking the profits each quarter, giving little thought to the future. Closures became commonplace throughout the 1950s and 1960s as cheaper imports – often woven on those same secondhand machines which had been bought from Britain – displaced home-produced textiles on the High Street.

But as with any industry, it was not simply those employed in the mills who lost their jobs. All the way down the supply chain – and far away from the 'dark satanic mills' themselves – thousands saw their livelihoods disappear. Those job losses had begun long before mills started closing, as the introduction of cardboard or plastic tubing replaced traditional wooden products such as bobbins.

Bobbin-making was an industry which employed large numbers of people from impoverished rural communities.

The scale of the demand for bobbins in Victorian times was enormous – in 1827, Samuel Crompton reckoned there were 4.6 million spindles in operation in Britain, each needing a steady supply of bobbins on to which the spun yarn would be wound. A century later, there were more than a million in use in Wigan, Lancashire, alone!

Bobbin-turning was a skill passed down through the generations, and was an important part of many local economies. In today's 'green' parlance, it was also entirely 'planet-friendly'. The wood was coppiced from sustainable sources, the mills were initially powered by water wheels, and the waste material was returned to nature. When steam engines were introduced, they were fuelled with the waste shavings from the workshop.

Locally grown ash, birch, sycamore oak, hazel, willow, field maple and sweet chestnut were all coppiced for a variety of uses, and many were used to make bobbins.

In the eighteenth century, bobbin turners worked in the woodlands they coppiced, many of them working small hand or foot-powered spindles to turn the coppiced wood into the ubiquitous bobbin. Output may have been relatively small, but demand was small too. But when the spinning industry expanded, and the weaving with it, demand for bobbins rose dramatically, and bobbin making had no choice but to become an industrial process itself.

Coppicing involves harvesting the new branches which grow from the stump – or stool – of a felled tree. These new shoots grow vigorously, and depending on the thickness of wood required, can produce a harvest every five to fifteen years. Some coppiced woods were used as fuel, others to make charcoal – essential for the early iron and steel industry – and in the west of Britain where the wetter climate produced very strong growth, coppiced woods were commonplace. Huge acreages of woodland were sustained to feed the seemingly insatiable demand from the charcoal burners and the bobbin-makers amongst others.

The great days of 'King Cotton' are long gone, remembered only in photographs and the few preserved mills we can visit today, but a tiny revival is possible. A company called English Fine Cottons – based in Tower Mill in Dukinfield, Greater Manchester which 140 years ago had boasted 44,000 spindles but which closed in 1955 – is seeking to re-establish that industry, albeit in a small way. They claim to be the only commercial cotton spinner operating in Britain.

Tower Mill, designed by one of Britain's leading mill architects – Edward Potts – is a Grade II listed building which managed to escape the wrecker's ball.

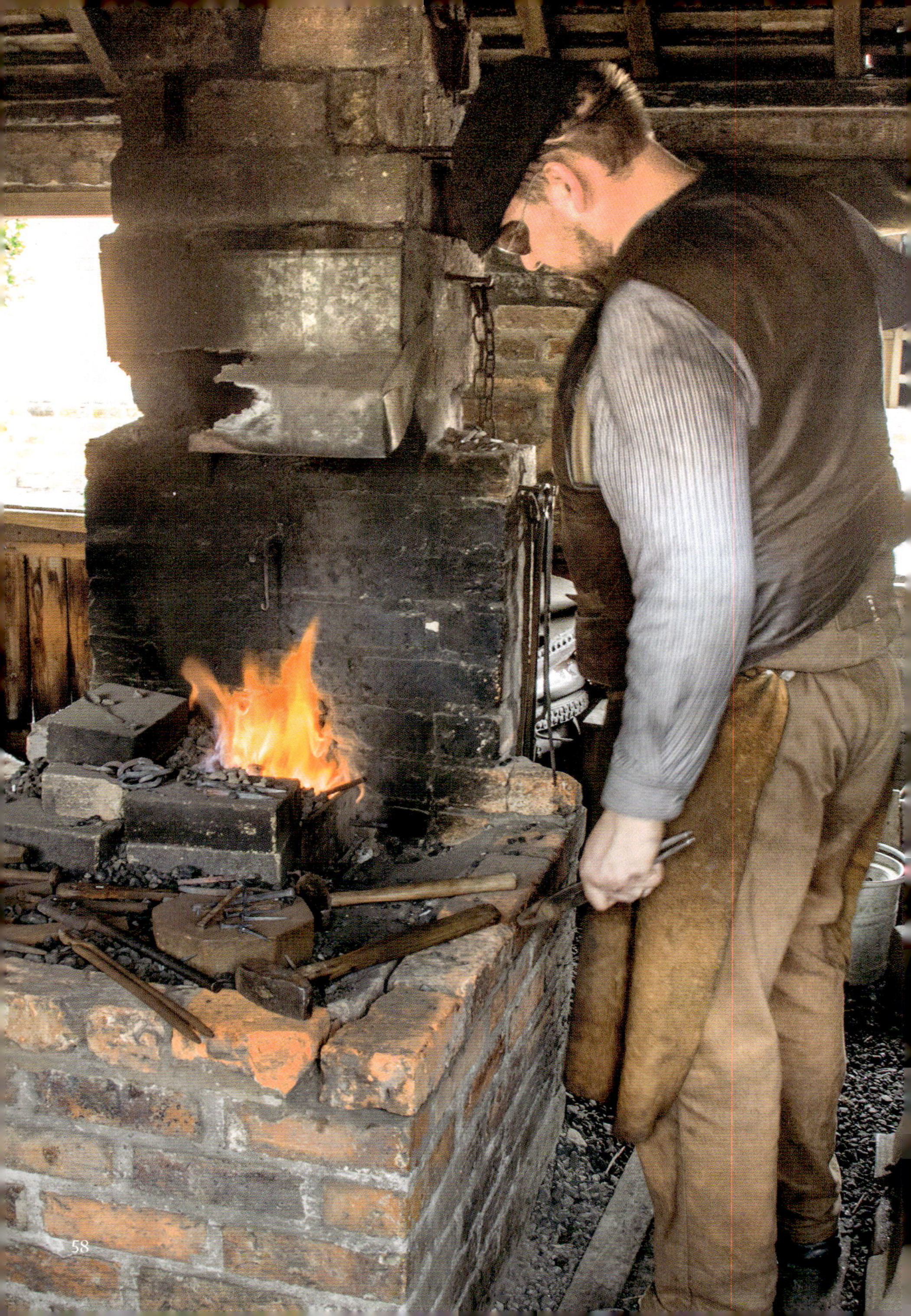

SICKLES, NEEDLES AND NAILS

MANUFACTURE MOVED RAPIDLY from small workshops to larger mills and factories in the eighteenth and nineteenth centuries. As the population of towns and cities grew, so did the need for housing, and that in turn increased demand for such basic things as nails – the making of which was once the exclusive province of the village blacksmith.

The construction of huge mills and factories to supply an ever-inceasing population with their everyday goods further increased the need for building materials, leading to the industrialisation of many manufacturing techniques.

Nail-making, however, with 'cut' nails made from iron bars, seems to have largely remained a hand craft for most of the nineteenth century – and that despite the introduction of machinery in the 1860s for the much faster manufacture of 'wire' nails. It is estimated that in the early years of Victoria's reign there were more than fifty thousand nail-makers at work in forges in the Black Country alone – most nails still hand-made.

Demonstrations of this onerous task can be seen in the recreation of a typical nail shop – *illustrated opposite* – originally established in Halesowen in the 1880s and now relocated to the Black Country Living Museum in Dudley.

When they were first imported into Britain, wire nails were referred to as 'French nails', although the machinery to make them had actually been pioneered in Belgium.

One of the first to begin the mass production of wire nails in Britain was Joseph Henry Nettleford in Smethwick in 1875 and the business he founded went on to become GKN, one of the leading industrial and aerospace components companies in Britain today.

above: The wooden and metal lift mechanism for the water-powered hammer and shears at Finch Foundry, Sticklepath, near Okehampton in Devon.

opposite page: A nail-maker at work in the restored Nail Shop at the Black Country Living Museum.

below: The techniques for making cut nails in the nineteenth century had changed very little since the Romans. These hand-made nails date from late mediaeval times.

AMONG THESE DARK SATANIC MILLS

SICKLES, NEEDLES AND NAILS

By the end of the nineteenth century, the manufacture of machine-made wire nails surpassed that of wrought iron nails for the first time, and the hand-worked rural nail forge, which had been in decline for decades, all but disappeared.

Very few examples of local industrial manufactures of small metal objects survive, but those which do are well worth exploration – amongst them Finch Foundry in Devon and Forge Mill Needle Museum in Redditch. Both are very rare survivors of once-common employers in their respective areas, and their preservation as working museums offers a vivid insight into the dangerous and labour-intensive manufacture of simple everyday objects.

Finch Foundry in Sticklepath near Okehampton, Devon, is a remarkable place, its primitive machinery having been used continuously by several generations of iron founders and blacksmiths until closure in 1960, after a wall collapse caused major structural damage and brought an end to almost 140 years under the ownership of the Finch family.

It occupies a site which has been in use for a variety of industrial purposes at least since mediaeval times, and up to the early nineteenth century the buildings had been used as a fulling mill, a woollen mill and a corn mill.

opposite page top: One of Finch Foundry's three overshot waterwheels. The site was restored by volunteers for North Dartmoor Museums and was given to the National Trust in 1994.

opposite bottom: Inside the foundry, the water-powered hammer and shears are a unique working survival, ably demonstrated by the Foundry's informed guides.

above: 'Artist Blacksmith' Andrew Kemp at work in Finch Foundry's smithy, forging a decorative poker for the author in 2019.

61

In 1814, when the Finch family took the site over, the woollen mill became the forge and the corn mill a grinding house. Trading as Finch Brothers, they described themselves variously as 'Edge Tool and Shovel Manufacturers', 'Agents for Batcheller's Hay and Manure Forks', 'Coal and General Merchants' and 'Factors and Importers of American Goods'.

'Edge Tools' was the term used to describe scythes, sickles and hay knives, manufactured using a forged sandwich of hardened steel between two layers of wrought iron. This was then heated and hammer-welded – using both drop-hammers and trip-hammers – to the required thickness before being ground to expose the steel core of the blade. Finch Foundry is the last remaining site in Britain where these water-powered hammers can be seen working.

The smaller hammer – weighing a mere 726 kilograms – could strike 240 times a minute. The larger hammer weighs over a tonne.

They were belt-driven from one of the mill's waterwheels, and at its peak, the foundry could produce around four hundred hand tools every day.

Today it looks much as it would have done around 1900, except it is a lot tidier and a lot quieter.

Even in some relatively large foundries, water-powered hammers survived well into the steam age – the workshops at Dinorwic Quarries in North Wales – now the Welsh

SICKLES, NEEDLES AND NAILS

National Slate Museum – being just one notable example.

But one of the major industrial developments was the introduction of the steam hammer.

First suggested by James Watt in his 1784 Patent for an improved steam engine – in which he described

> 'Heavy Hammers or Stampers, for forging or stamping iron, copper, or other metals, or other matters without the intervention of rotative motions or wheels, by fixing the Hammer or Stamper to be so worked, either directly to the piston or piston rod of the engine'

The idea was developed by fellow Scotsman James Nasmyth in 1839 – in direct response to the need to forge the enormous paddle shaft for Isambard Kingdom Brunel's transatlantic steamship the SS *Great Britain* then under construction at Bristol.

By the time Nasmyth had designed a big enough hammer, Brunel had made the decision to convert the ship to propeller drive, so the paddle shaft was abandoned.

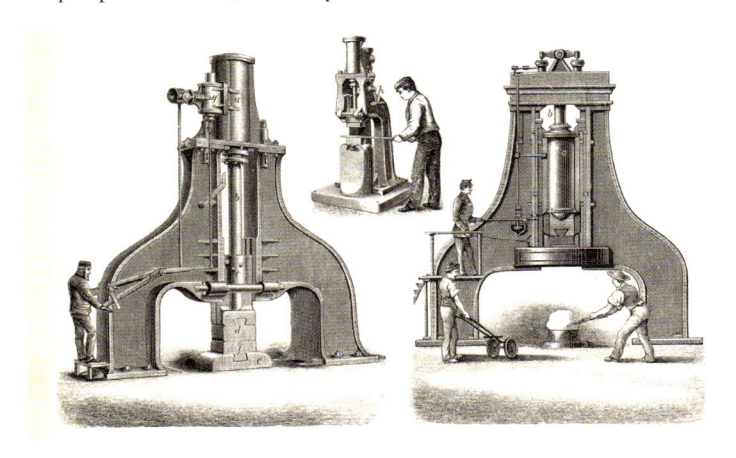

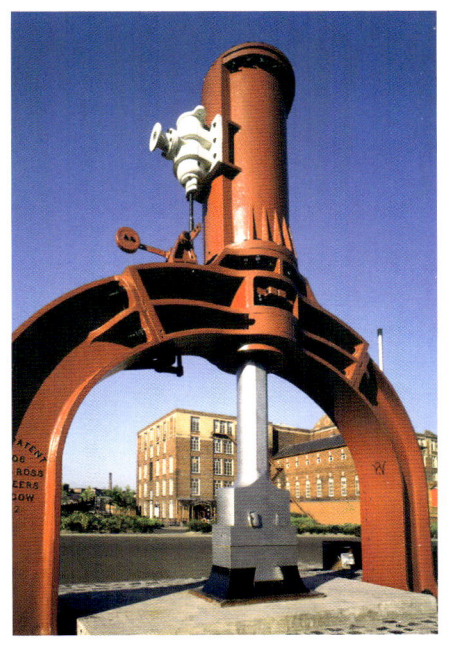

opposite top: The Thwaites belt-driven hammer at Dinorwic.

opposite bottom: A modified pneumatic hammer by B & G Massey of Manchester, also at Dinorwic.

above: This large William Rigby designed steam hammer was built in 1862 by Glen and Ross of Glasgow and was one of three installed at William Parks & Company's Clarington Forge in Wigan, Lancashire.

left: A late nineteenth century illustration of large steam hammers.

Throughout the nineteenth century, hammers driven by water, steam and compressed air were to be found in thousands of foundries and factories throughout the country.

Very few examples of local industrial enterprises survive, but another one which has been saved has been re-assembled in the unique and aptly-named Museum of Bath at Work.

When we visit a World Heritage Site like Bath, with its Roman Baths, mediaeval abbey and beautiful Georgian streets and crescents, it is easy to lose sight of the fact that Bath was, like any other, a working city with a significant industrial past.

One of its many entrepreneurs was Jonathan Bowler. He was an accomplished engineer who had acquired his skills the hard way, having been apprenticed in 1848 – at the age of fourteen – to N. G Wilcocks' Bath City Brass Foundry & Iron Works at 44-46 Avon Street. One of their successful product ranges was water aeration machinery for the growing fizzy drinks industry.

above: The stores at Dirnowic Quarries – the company prided itself on being able to manufacture and repair almost everything it needed, and to achieve that had extensive stores of spare parts, screws, bolts and other essentials.

below: J. B. Bowler's premises on Bath's Corn Street shortly before demolition.

above: Bowler's recreated machine shop as it looks from above today. The interior was recreated from photographs of the original premises, and the machinery is now operated by electricity on request.

While still in his twenties Bowler had become the foundry foreman, but some time around 1864 and with the agreement of his employers, he started building up a lucrative part-time business in his own time – describing himself as a blacksmith, a gas fitter, and a brass founder amongst other skills, and slowly building up a clientele making small metal objects, repairing broken gates, and taking on small engineering jobs.

In early 1872 he took the decision to leave the City Brass Foundry and open his own factory, trading as J. B. Bowler & Sons, manufacturing brass pipes, tubes and valves.

Amongst the machinery they built was equipment for the soft drinks industry – building on the skills he had learned as an apprentice. Unusually, this was with the full agreement of his former employers, and as time went on, they even started sub-contracting work to him.

Rather than working in competition the two businesses, one long established, the other brand new, worked in concert, and Bowler and Wilcocks remained friends and business colleagues until Wilcocks's death.

Having produced and successfully marketed his aeration machines worldwide, Bowler expanded into the premises

right: Tools on the repair shop bench at J. B. Bowler's works, reassembled in Museum of Bath at Work. It just looks as though the workers have briefly stepped outside.

round the corner in Corn Street and started making his own fizzy drinks using some of the machines himself, opening up a new aspect to his business.

It proved to be a highly successful one. Generations of Bath's residents enjoyed Bowler's ginger beers, fruit cordials and 'orange champagne'.

Also in Corn Street were the engineering works of Samuel Griffin, designer of several patented steam – and later gas and oil – engines. Bowler and Griffin were friends so it was logical that it would be Griffin who supplied steam engines to the business once the mineral water business began in 1876. That first steam engine survives.

Later, as demand for power increased in both the foundry and the aeration plant, more powerful oil engines took over, continuing in use until electricity was installed.

Griffin did not have the manufacturing capacity to build and market his larger engines and so, while retaining his interests in his patents, he assigned manufacturing rights to Dick, Kerr & Company of Kilmarnock.

Amongst the engines Griffin designed, and Dick Kerr manufactured, was a powerful six-stroke engine built in 1883 – Griffin's patented modification of Nikolaus August Otto's four-stroke gas engine, introduced in Germany in 1878 – which was supplied to the Gas Light and Coke Company's Beckton Gasworks in London, said to have been the largest gas works in Europe.

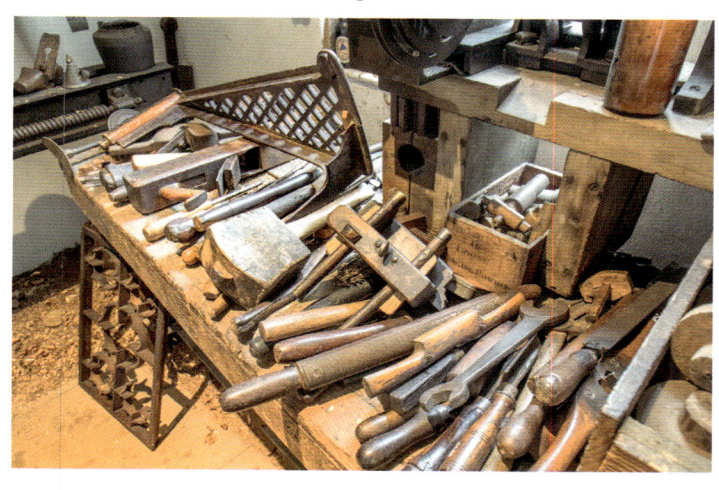

SICKLES, NEEDLES AND NAILS

left: The laboratory in Bowler's fizzy drinks factory.

middle: Bowlers would undertake just about any repair job, from mending beer pumps to welding gates — in addition to their manufacturing base next door.

bottom left: A vintage Imperial typewriter on Mr Bowler's desk in the factory office.

bottom right: An 1852 prize-winning pressure gauge by Barnett, Son & Foster of London is displayed in the drinks factory, and lists the bottling pressures for a wide range of popular fizzy drinks — from 40 inches of pressure for champagne to 140 inches for soda water.

67

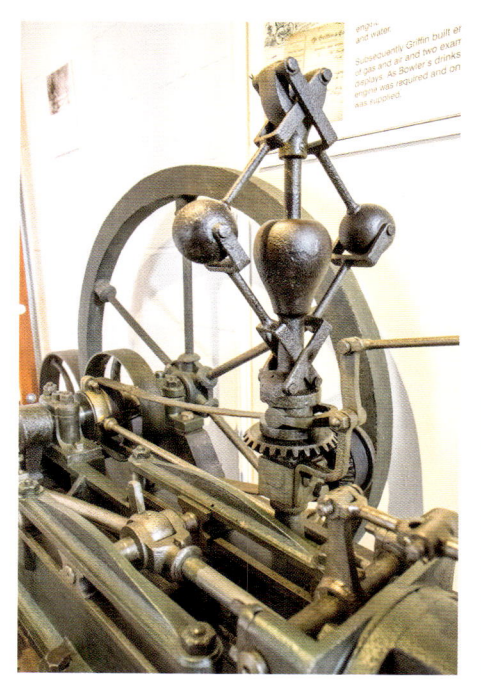

above: This small 1876 steam engine by Griffin of Bath was the first to be acquired by Jonathan Bowler to drive the machinery in his fizzy drinks plant.

above right: The Griffin engine drove this carbonated water pump, a task later taken over by a larger gas engine, also made by Griffin.

The engine was finally withdrawn from service in 1956 after seventy-three years' service. Two examples of this unusual design are known to survive.

Jonathan Bowler was a bit of a hoarder, never throwing anything away lest it might prove useful at some later date – a trait he instilled into his children as well.

Thus the shop, foundry, and the drinks factory next door all became somewhat cluttered over the years – but while everything in shops around them was being sold 'pre-packaged', Bowler's remained the sort of place where you could still buy a pound of nails or a couple of washers.

Sadly, the era of such businesses had passed long before Bowler's ceased trading in 1969 – scheduled for demolition to make way for the Avon Street multi-storey car park – but by a fortuitous twist of fate, the premises and their contents were not destined to go the way of so many others.

A local businessman recognised the treasure-trove which lay behind the doors of Bowler's Corn Street premises, and acquired the total contents. Inside was the Victorian foundry and bottling works, largely unchanged for three quarters of a century, tools laid down on benches as if the workforce had merely clocked off for the night.

Rescuing shops, mills and other enterprises for posterity, preserving snapshots of our past, is what has driven the creation of 'heritage towns' such as the Beamish Open Air Museum in Northumberland, Blists Hill near Telford and the Black Country Living Museum in Dudley. On all three sites, premises have been carefully dismantled and re-erected on site, usually around a few surviving examples of the industries which did actually once provide employment in those areas. In the case of the Black Country Living Museum, it was the Dudley Canal and its lime kilns; at both Beamish and Blists Hill it was the coal mines and ironworks which formed the nuclei of the new 'old towns'.

In these 'living museums' it is now possible to watch craftsmen making all sort of items using techniques which became obsolete a century and more ago.

In addition to the nail-maker discussed at the beginning of this chapter, the Black Country Living Museum also invites visitors to see how chains were forged by hand – back-breaking work, undertaken by workers who were paid simply by the total weight of their day's labours. Thus someone making small chain links had to work flat out to earn a living, while, as the chain-maker pointed out, someone making the anchor chain for the RMS *Titanic* – where each link, made out of iron bar with a five inch diameter, weighed

below: Part of the rolling mill, formerly at Thomas Walmsley's Atlas Forge in Bolton. Opened in 1866, the forge lasted until 1975 when it was the last plant in the United Kingdom to produce wrought iron. It once had sixteen furnaces. After closure, the rolling mill was re-erected in the Blists Hill Victorian Town, part of the Ironbridge Gorge Museums near Telford, Shropshire.

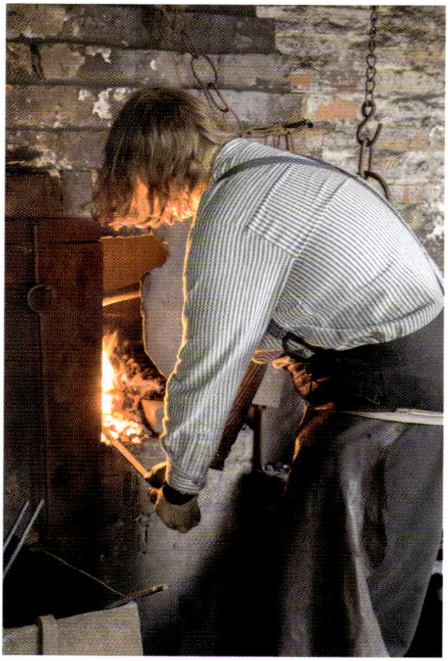

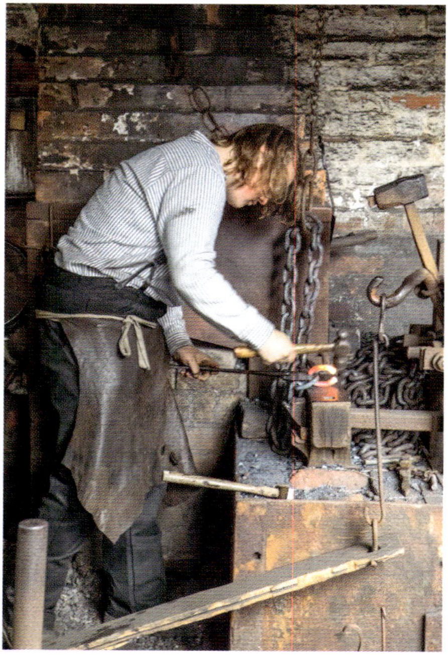

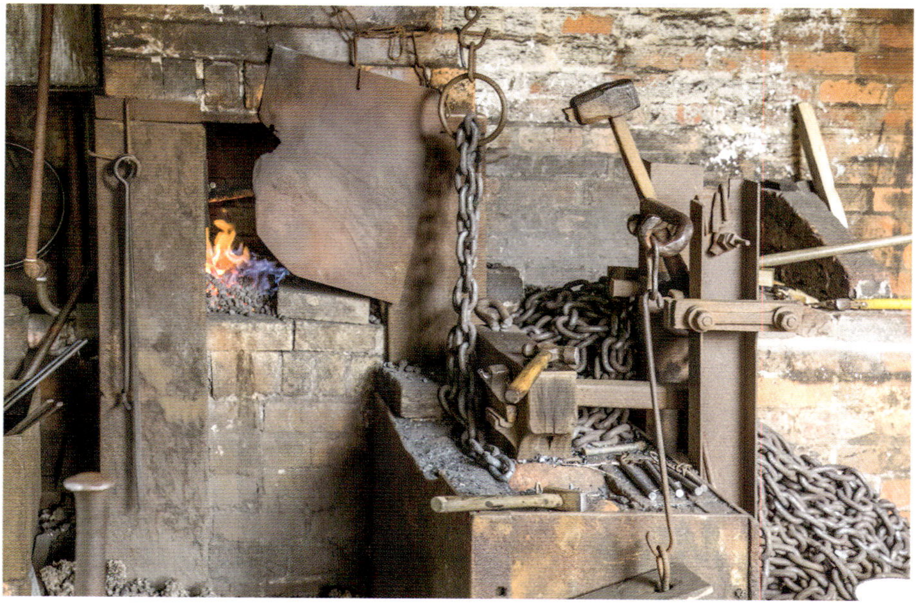

SICKLES, NEEDLES AND NAILS

nearly a quarter of a ton – would have to work as part of a well-disciplined team to make even a single link. Links on that scale, of course, were shaped using enormous steam hammers rather than hand tools.

The steam hammer at the Museum was built in the late nineteenth century by Charles Ross of Sheffield, and is currently undergoing restoration to return it to operation.

In Redditch in the eighteenth and nineteenth centuries, the manufacture of some very small objects – needles – was on a massive scale. Within a 10 mile radius of the town, most of the world's needles were once manufactured – needles for everything from the home dress-maker and the world's gramophones up to huge needles for a variety of industrial processes such as carpet-making.

The last surviving working needle mill – Forge Mill – is now a fascinating museum, revealing the truly awful conditions under which such simple objects were made.

One of the worst health hazards was said to be 'Pointer's Rot', which we know today as silicosis.

above: The steam hammer from Anchor Forge, now at the Black Country Living Museum, dressed for a 'Peaky Blinders' special event.

Opposite from top left: The chain-maker at work in the Black Country Living Museum – a fascinating insight and demonstration into chain-making from the relatively small to the huge links which were used to make the anchor chains on the RMS *Titanic*.

opposite bottom: The chain-maker's workshop.

right: Forge Mill Needle Museum in Redditch is the last surviving example of a needle mill in Britain,

middle: The Skimming Machine in the mill removed scale from the needles, and this example is said to date from around 1900. It was built by Edward White of Redditch for the Ashleigh Works in Bromsgrove Road, a short distance from White's factory.

below: Hooked needles were used in the Leicester-made Victoria Sock-Knitting Machine, popular in the early twentieth century. Machines like these were given to disabled ex-servicemen after the Great War so they could earn a living. They could make up to 18 pairs a day. The example *below* is displayed in Forge Mill and *below right* in Shetland's Tangwick Haa Museum.

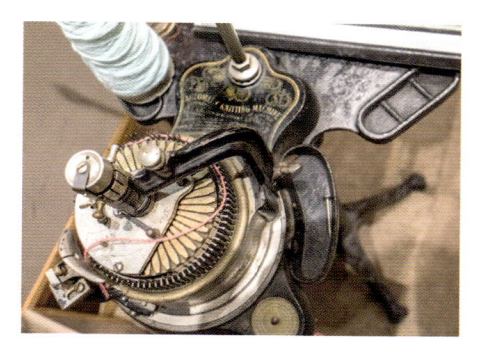

SICKLES, NEEDLES AND NAILS

top: The nineteenth century scouring machinery at Forge Mill. Needles to be scoured were tightly packed into what were known as 'setts' — made up of strips of canvas and hessian. Up to 60,000 needles were packed into a 'sett' with grease, scouring agents such as emery power, and soft soap. Each sett was put underneath one of the 'scouring runners' which were driven by the mill's waterwheel. The scouring process could last anything from a day to a week.

left: The scoured needles were washed and then placed in rotating barrels for twenty minutes, mixed with hot sawdust to dry them.

below: One of the many elaborate needle cases on display in the museum. Several designs of needle case were protected by patents.

The men who pointed the needles – and it was predominantly men for that task – were very well paid but worked in clouds of dust from the needles themselves and the grinding tools, damaging their eyes and lungs. After two to three years, many were coughing blood, and very few lasted more than ten years. The average life expectancy of a needle pointer in the early nineteenth century was said to be just thirty-five years.

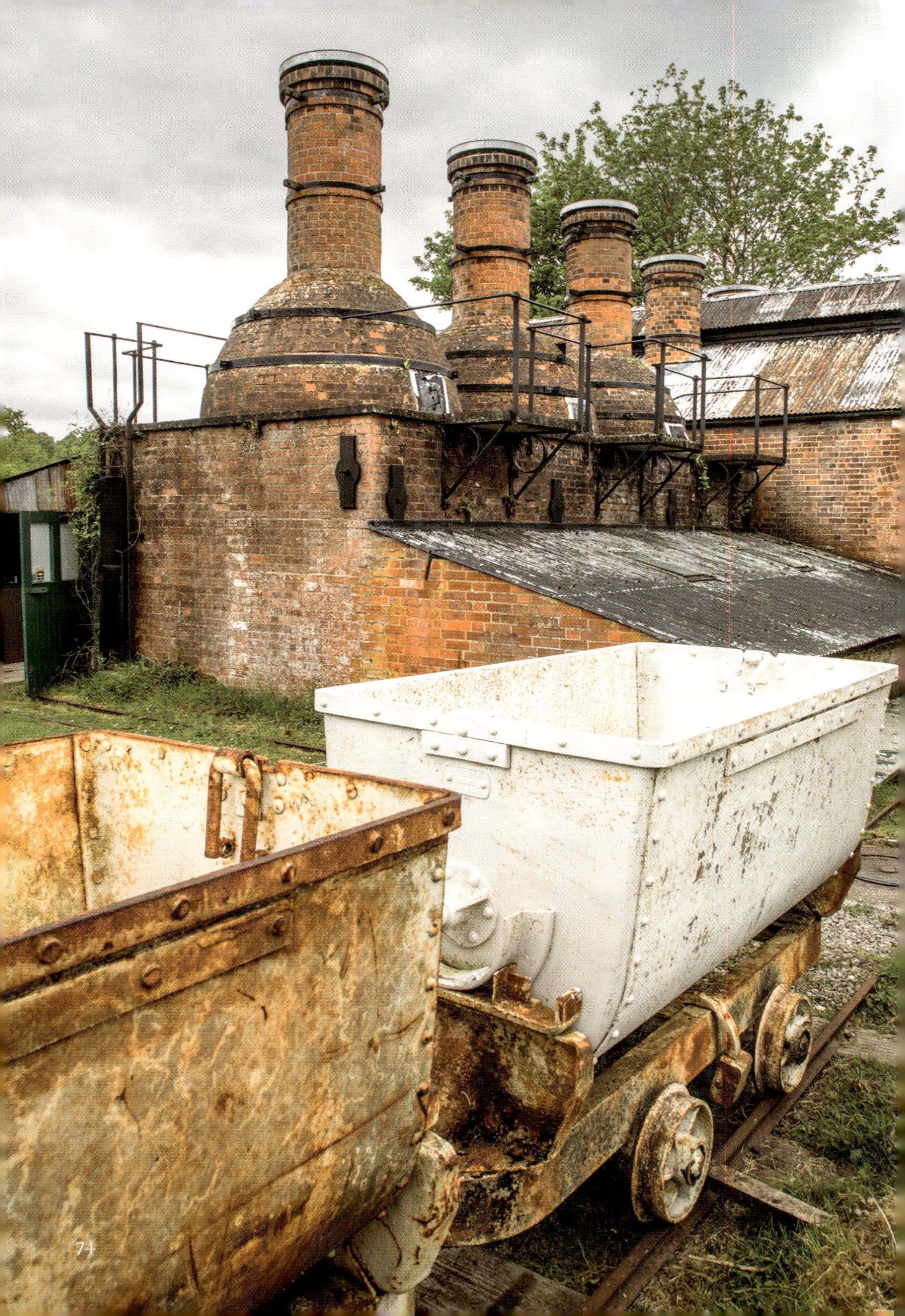

A LUST FOR LIME

TWYFORD WATERWORKS, just a few miles south of Winchester in Hampshire, is an amazing survival. The buildings house, amongst other things, a massive Hathorn Davey & Company steam pumping engine installed in 1914 to replace the larger of a pair of beam engines which had been installed in 1899 by Day, Summers & Co of Southampton. The new engine pumped 11 million litres of water per day from the aquifers deep beneath the site. The smaller beam engine had been replaced in 1905 by a triple expansion engine built at Richardsons, Westgarth & Company's Hartlepool Engine Works.

The first well on site was sunk in 1898, the second in 1899, and the two beam engines initially shared the work – the larger one raising the water from the well, the smaller one pumping it 54 metres up the hill to a holding reservoir.

By the time the two triple expansion engines were in place – each fitted with two pumps – they shared the operations so that if one had to be shut down for any reason, the entire operation could continue with the other. The reservoirs

opposite: Twyford Waterworks is unique in Britain, having its own water-softening plant on site, including the lime kilns which supplied the raw materials. The five limekilns were served by a narrow-gauge railway running around the site.

below: Twyford Pumping Station seen from the lime kilns.

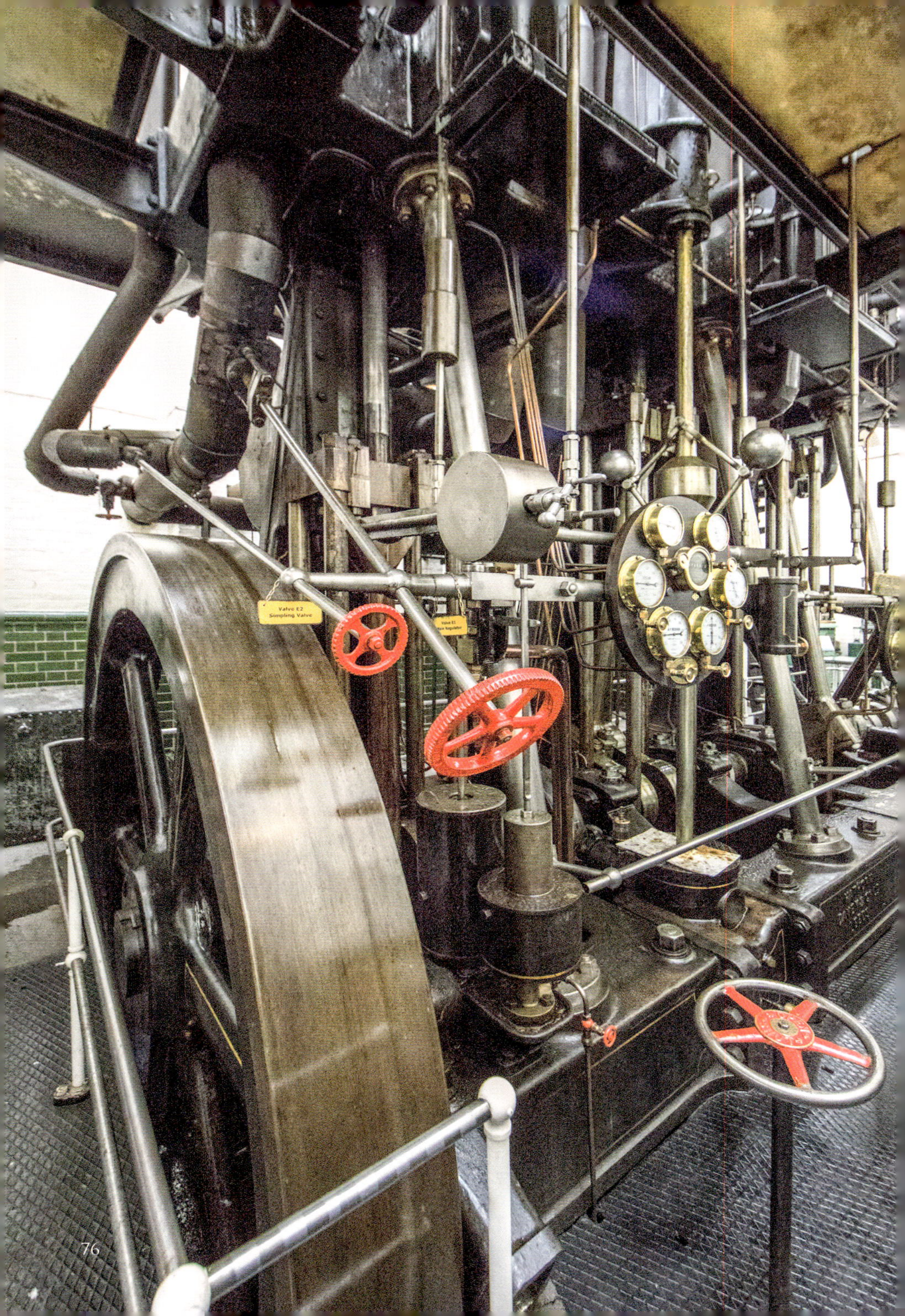
Valve E2
Simpling Valve
Valve E1

originally just held one day's supply of water, so a break in supply would have caused real problems.

When first opened, the pumping station raised around two million litres a day, but by the end of the Edwardian era it had reached the maximum daily quantity permitted by its 1910 Act of Parliament – 11 million litres, or two and a half million gallons in old money.

Twyford Waterworks has another, unique, aspect which makes it all the more interesting.

Most of Britain has hard water – the major exceptions being the Lake District and the Pennines. The area covering much of Wiltshire and Hampshire is predominantly chalk (limestone), and the aquifers within the chalk hold water in vast quantities. Sinking wells into the chalk seemed to provide the Victorian water engineers of Hampshire with an almost limitless source of pure, clean water, but with a bit of a problem – it is incredibly hard water containing a lot of dissolved calcium carbonate.

It furs up pipes and taps; boil it and it scales up kettles; use it for washing clothes or dishes and it causes soap to scum. In other words, while it tastes good and is very good for one's health, it has to be softened before it is of much use for other domestic purposes.

opposite: The massive pumping engine at Twyford Waterworks, built by Hathorn Davey of Leeds, which delivered fresh water to the ciy of Winchester in Hampshire. Improving supplies of fresh water was a key component of Britain's industrial progress in Victorian times. The engine is regularly steamed throughout the summer months.

left: The interior of the kilnhouse, known as the 'charging floor'. The charging doors would be bricked up once the kilns had been filled with coal and chalk.

above: Twyford's mixing room where lime and water were combined to create 'slaked lime' which was then added to the freshly pumped water.

It is in the method used to resolve that problem that Twyford Waterworks is unique. It is the only preserved waterworks in the country which still has its own on-site water softening plant in situ – although no longer in everyday use – giving us the opportunity to explore an innovative Victorian solution to an age-old problem.

The chalk rocks which store the water, are themselves an essential ingredient in the process of water softening known as the Clark Process.

Dr Thomas Clark (1801-1867) was a Scottish-born chemist who became Professor of Chemistry at Aberdeen's Marischal College in 1833. Amongst his notable achievements were the establishment of standards and tests by which the 'hardness' of water could be measured and, of course, the Clark Process of water softening – first used to soften and clean Thames water in 1854. The type of hardness the process could deal with is known as 'temporary hardness', and is caused by high concentrations of carbonates in the water. Remove those carbonates – by chemically converting them into sludge – and the hard water becomes softer.

Clark's classification system identified the 'hardness' of Lake District water being below 2 degrees of hardness on his scale. Hampshire water is rated as 19 degrees, with Lee Valley water in London a little higher.

Hardly surprising, then, that the first area to experiment with Clark's softening system was in London – the East London Waterworks Company in Walthamstow, which was opened in 1853, was one of eight private water companies in London at the time.

Clark's process was an extension of the age-old task of converting the chalky stone into lime. The locally-mined limestone – calcium carbonate – was fed into a kiln – Twyford has five of them – with alternate layers of coal and chalk, where over a period of a couple of days the intense heat would break it down into quicklime – calcium oxide – which can be raked out at the foot of the kiln.

Mixed with water, it then becomes calcium hydroxide – 'slaked lime' – and is added, in carefully measured concentrations, to the water being pumped up from the aquifer and fed into the softening tank. The calcium carbonate is precipitated out and the now softer water is fed through filters to remove any other impurities before being pumped up to reservoirs ready for distribution to the people of Winchester.

This was, however, a rather inefficient operation as the kilns were only fired up when fresh supplies of lime were needed. That wasted a lot of fuel, as well as shortening the useful life of the firebricks inside the kilns by repeated heating and cooling. Despite its inefficiencies, the system supplied the all waterworks' lime from 1903 until 1969.

Softening water, however, is but a tiny fraction of the many uses mankind has found for lime. Its uses in agriculture can be traced back thousands of years, and the remains of thousands of ancient limekilns can still be seen dotted across the landscape.

Many were sited on the coast, or on river estuaries so that the raw materials, if not available locally, could be brought in by boat, and the finished lime transported away to customers by the same means.

The trade in lime was extensive, some users needing massive quantities for industrial purposes, others small

below: Beadnell Limekilns on the Northumberland coast were sited at the edge of the harbour – ideal for bringing chalk in by boat and shipping lime out the same way.

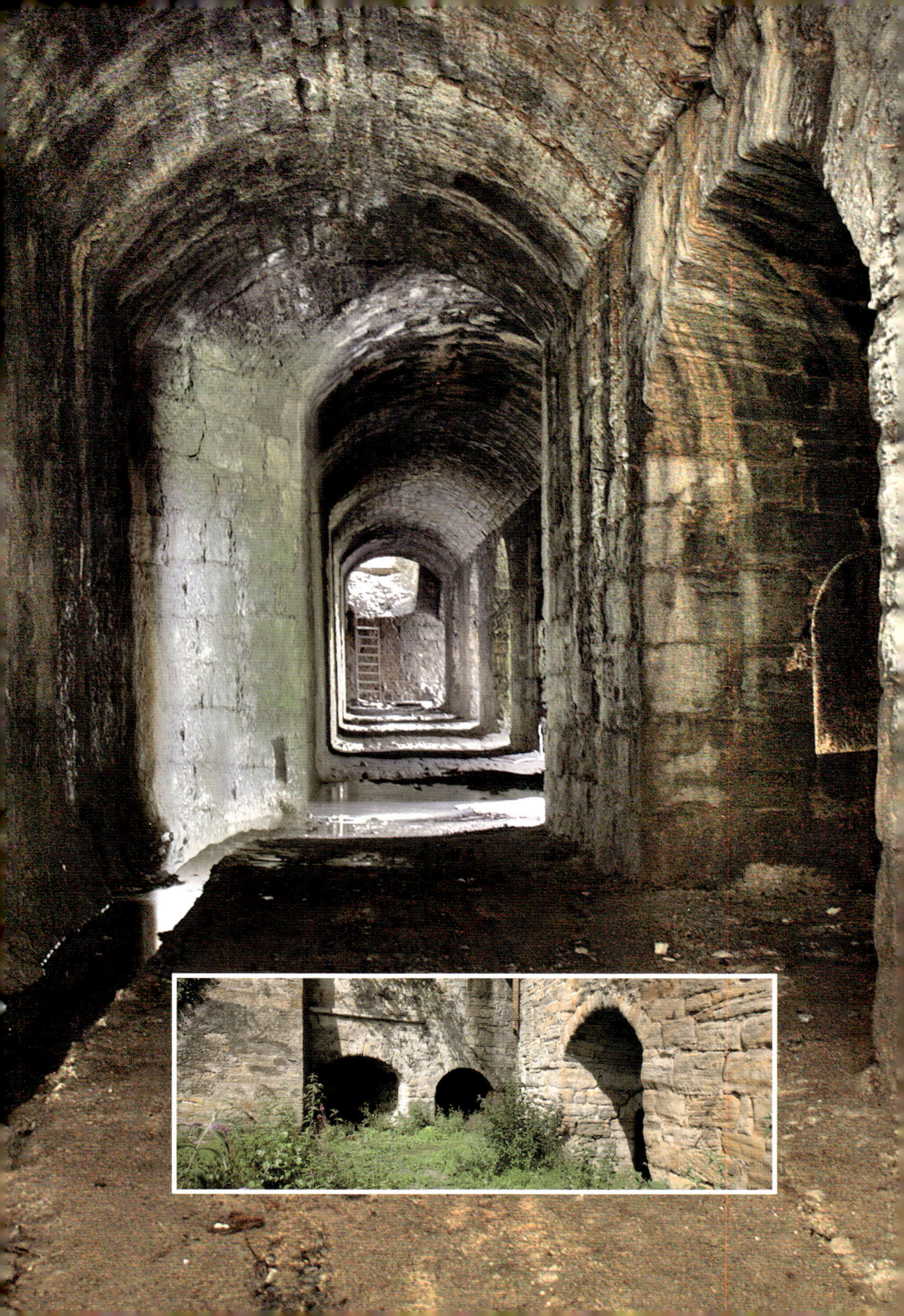

A LUST FOR LIME

left: The limekiln at Clovelly, Devon, 1895. Quicklime was made here from the fourteenth century until the nineteenth. Limestone and culm — low quality anthracite — for the kilns was shipped across the Bristol Channel from South Wales. The kilns are still standing.

below: A bill of sale from Hetton Lime Kilns in Northumberland, dated December 1825. The kilns, of which some remains survive, were a relatively small-scale operation, probably just supplying local demands. The 24 Bolls of Lime covered by this receipt were sold to landowner Sir Horace St Paul who lived at Ewart Park nearby.

amounts to spread on fields. In agriculture, lime reduced the acidity of soil and raised both potassium and calcium levels, essential for plant growth.

Interestingly, the weights and measures used by suppliers varied from region to region. In Scotland and the North East of England, for example, lime was sold using an old mediaeval measure known as the 'boll'. A boll could be a measure of weight or a measure of volume – for dry goods such as lime, a boll weighed in at around 140lbs.

As a vital constituent of mortar, its use in construction helped shape some of the finest buildings from Roman times – a lime-based concrete was used to build the Pantheon in Rome, and lime plaster has been used on walls for well over

opposite page: Inside the limekilns at Charlestown on the Firth of Forth. Heat, smoke and dust made working conditions atrocious, especially for those whose work was to constantly stoke the furnaces in the semi-darkness of tunnels like this. An open furnace door can be seen to the right of the passageway. Since this view was taken, long overdue work on conserving the site has been initiated.

right: Lime mortar and lime plaster are surprisingly durable and flexible materials. On the tower walls at St Giles church in Imber on Salisbury Plain, are the sequences for ringing a full peal of bells, dating from 1692, the most complete survival of such a chart in the country.

below right: Lime plaster being used in the restoration of Imber church. Some of the wall paintings have been dated to 1280.

below: Decorative plasterwork at the eighteenth-century House of Dun near Montrose in Scotland, now cared for by the National Trust for Scotland.

ten thousand years. Lime plaster's suitability as a surface on which to apply rich decoration is celebrated in great buildings from Roman Pompeii to the present day.

Across Britain, lime plaster was used to create magnificent moulded decoration in great houses – with some remarkable Jacobean and Rococco examples surviving.

Lime was – and still is – a vital component in so many industrial processes, but in the eighteenth century it was in huge demand for making mortar for the building trade as Britain sought to build new industrial cities and house those who were moving in from the countryside in search of work.

The eighteenth-century traveller, Thomas Pennant, believed he had seen one of the industrial marvels of the age when he visited Charles Bruce, Earl of Elgin in 1772, and saw his limekilns near the village of Charlestown on the shores of the River Forth.

Originally opened in the 1750s, they were still being expanded in number and output when Pennant visited. He had never seen anything like them. They epitomised industrial progress and were, he said,

> 'the greatest perhaps in the universe, placed amidst inexhaustible beds of limestone, and near immense seams of coal.'

The kilns were so vast that it is said to have taken more than two weeks for the limestone to make its way to the bottom of the furnaces and be raked out as lime.

Intriguingly, just along the shore is the village of Limekilns where relatively small-scale production was centuries-old, but it was at Charlestown that the process was developed onto the massive industrial scale which so impressed eighteenth-century visitors.

Most lime kilns were like vast upturned bottles made of brick – wide at the top and tapering towards the bottom. They were continuously loaded from the top with alternate layers of chalk and coal, and by the time the mixture reached the bottom, it had pretty well all been converted into lime. The few lumps which remained were ground into powder.

above: The ornate late seventeenth-century plaster ceiling in the drawing room at Astley Hall in Lancashire.

IN DARK SATANIC MILLS

above: Two of the De Witt kilns at Amberley have been preserved.

above right: The De Witt kilns were replaced by inverted bottle kilns, after which horses and carts fed chalk and coal into them from above.

middle: A grinding mill was used at the No.1 Kilns to break up any lumps of limestone which reached the bottom.

right: A narrow-gauge railway moved the chalk to the kilns. The green wagons were props for scenes for the 1985 James Bond film *A View to a Kill* which were filmed at the museum.

A LUST FOR LIME

above: Although only two of the surviving kilns are to De Witt's design, the huge building at Amberley is still known as the De Witt Kilns.

left: The No. 2 kilns were built around the same time as the De Witts, but to a conventional design. The inverted-bottle-shaped chambers are 23 feet (7.5 metres) deep and were fed from the top. These kilns were fuelled and filled continuously — the major damage done to a kiln is caused by repeated heating and cooling, causing expansion and contraction of the fire bricks inside.

At Amberley in West Sussex, rare examples of 'De Witt' kilns survive, invented by a Belgian brick-maker, Hippolyte De Witt and introduced on to the site in 1904.

His kilns look more like brick kilns than lime kilns, and were loaded from the front, combustion requiring a strong down-draught from above the burning chamber, rather than the up-draught used in conventional lime-burning.

85

above: The mouth of one of the furnaces at Blaenafon Ironworks. These furnaces were only shut down when the lining of fire bricks needed to be replaced. There would have been a local brickworks which manufactured the fire bricks.

right: The furnaces at Blaenafon Ironworks were fed round the clock from the top with iron ore, limestone and coal — the operating temperature was around 1000°C. The limestone acted as a flux, helping keep the molten iron clear of impurities.

The design anticipated that the combustion gases would be drawn down through the fire and vented up a tall chimney flue. Sadly, while de Witt's design may have worked well when firing bricks, it was a very inefficient way of converting chalk into lime, and within six years they had been rebuilt as conventional kilns – but the block is still known to this day as the 'De Witt Kilns'.

The Amberley kilns have been stabilised and partially restored thanks to a Heritage Lottery Fund grant. Two of them are displayed as De Witt designed them.

Since the images of Charlestown in this book were taken, Fife Council and the National Trust for Scotland have undertaken a partial restoration of the site. All the undergrowth has been removed, revealing much more of the sheer scale of the works, and it is hoped this will result in much better public access in the future.

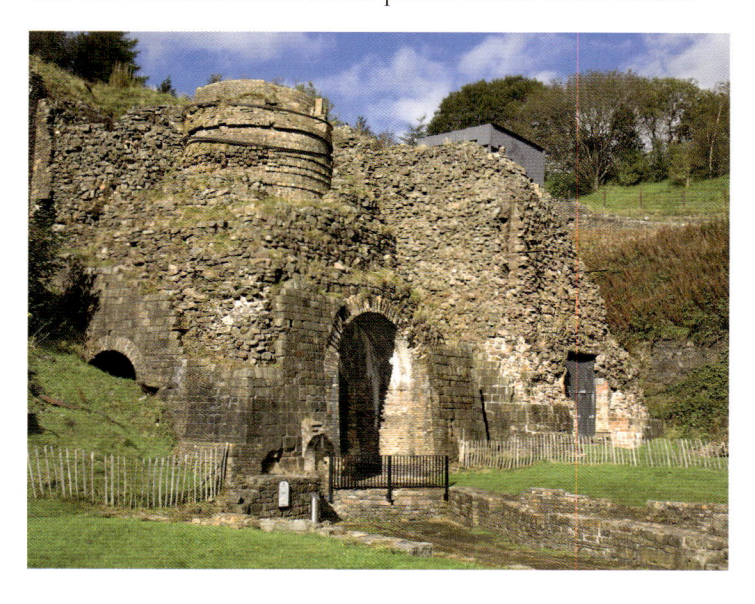

Lime was also a key ingredient in the smelting of iron from ore – it acted as a flux in the large furnaces, removing impurities and slag from the liquid metal.

The surviving blast furnaces at Blaenafon Ironworks in South Wales hint at the awful working conditions.

Round the clock workers raised huge quantities of coal or coke, iron ore and limestone to the upper level of the works where they were tipped into the tops of the voracious blast furnaces.

These furnaces rarely went out – unless repairs and maintenance were needed – so the raw materials were being tipped into the tops of the searingly hot stacks, belching smoke and gases, and often propelling small clouds of burning gas up into the air. The work must have been exhausting, terrifying for the young apprentices, and very dangerous. The young women who broke up the limestone before it was tipped into the inferno had it easy by comparison.

A well-preserved set of limekilns can be seen at the Black Country Living Museum in Dudley. So important was lime to the local economy that these kilns were built with their own specially-constructed branch of the Dudley Canal, linking them to the Birmingham Canal Navigation and thus the industrial heartlands of the Midlands.

The kilns were built in 1842 – nearly ninety years after Lord Elgin's Charlestown Kilns – underlining the fact that demand for lime was still on the increase.

The Dudley Canal itself had been open for fifty years before the spur to the limekilns was completed, and the kilns themselves continued to be worked well into the 1920s.

While many of the limekilns dotted across the landscape are simple and rudimentary affairs – some large, most small – a few were built with the same attention to architectural detail usually reserved for great houses and churches.

above: Nowhere is the water-solubility of limestone more apparent than on the so-called 'limestone pavements' which can be found in Britain and Ireland. Limestone is already slightly soluble in water – hence 'hard water' – but it is especially soluble in acidic rainwater. So over time, the limestone, initially exposed by receding glaciers, has been dissolved away at its weakest points – cracks. The resulting slabs are known as 'clints', the fissures 'grykes'. This is Malham Cove, one of Yorkshire's best known beauty spots.

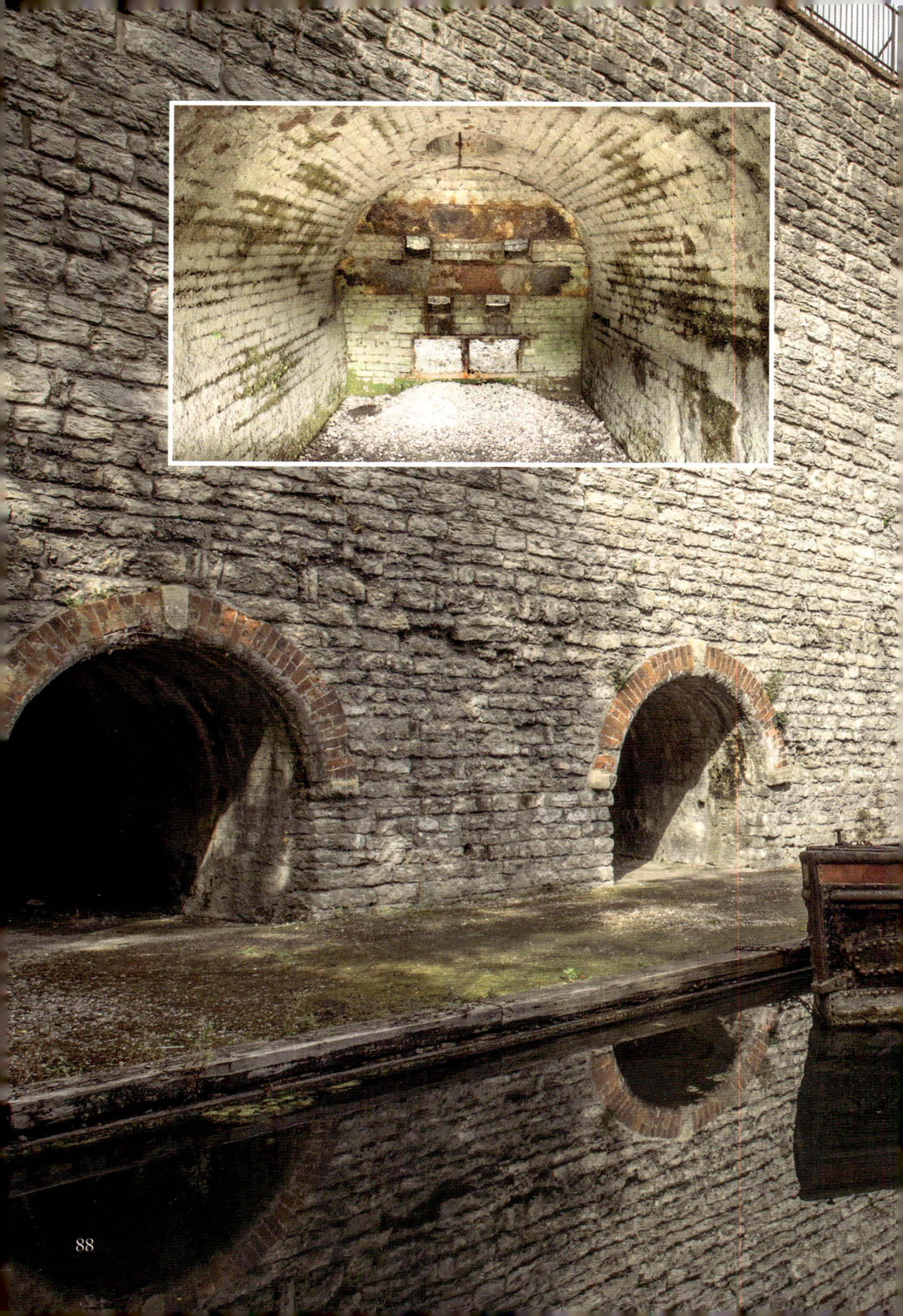

A LUST FOR LIME

The **Limekilns on the Dudley Canal spur**, now part of the Black Country Living Museum, operated from 1842 until the 1920s. Limestone was fed in at the top of the furnaces, and by the time it reached the bottom, the constant heat of the fires had converted it into lumps of quicklime. Men, or boys, prodded the lumps of quicklime through the four holes in the end wall of the kiln to break it into much smaller pieces which were then raked out through the two holes in the bottom. It was a continuous process, and the working conditions for the men in each of the six kiln mouths must have been atrocious, the heat and the lime dust resulting in severe damage to the workers' lungs and eyes.

right and below left: Decorative lime plaster motifs, displayed in the premises of E. Biddulph, Decorative Plasterers, now re-erected in Blists Hill Victorian Town – one of the Ironbridge Gorge Museums.

below right: In the nineteenth century, in the days before mains electricity was commonplace, 'limelight' was used to light theatres and music halls, and to provide the light source for magic lantern projectors. The pipes coming out of the back of the projector were for the oxygen and hydrogen supplies which heated a rotatable block of quicklime.

An especially impressive survival is to be found in Llandybie in Carmarthenshire – the Cilyrychen Lime Kilns, designed by the eminent Welsh ecclesiastical architect, Richard Kyrke Penson, were constructed in the Victorian Gothic style between 1856 and 1858, and there were originally six kilns. A further six were added in later phases, but in a much more utilitarian style.

Penson's church-building background is obvious. Despite having several churches to his name, he had never designed industrial buildings before, which makes his choice as architect for the Llandybie project all the more surprising. Looking at the kilns today, it is hard to imagine that his beautifully constructed cathedral-like buildings, built for just under £3500, served such a utilitarian purpose.

Today, such structures would have been in a style – if we can call it that – as utilitarian as the purpose they served, but to our Victorian forefathers, the appearance of a building was considered important, leaving us with the many impressive factories and mills on the heritage trails we follow today. No other kilns looked like these, however.

By 1900 there were nine kilns at Llandybie, standing 50 feet high and between them they could produce 20 tons of lime a day. The site continued to be used for lime production until 1973.

Today lime is still extensively used in the iron and steel industries, and is an essential lubricant in the manufacture of aluminium, steel and copper wire, and other metal products. In some industrial countries this use of lime products has overtaken its use in mortars and plasters.

It is also used in the manufacture of glass, paper, and even some plastics. Demand shows no sign of abating.

Lime manufacture these days, however, is on a massive commercial scale, leaving no room for the hundreds – perhaps thousands – of small local producers, the remains of whose kilns can still be seen across the country.

below: Despite being a scheduled monument, Richard Kyrke Penson's spectacular Victorian Gothic cathedral-like Cilyrychen Lime Kilns at Llandybie in south-west Wales, the six of which shown here were opened in 1858, are slowly being reclaimed by nature. A site like this deserves conservation to prevent further deterioration, and should not be fenced off and inaccessible.

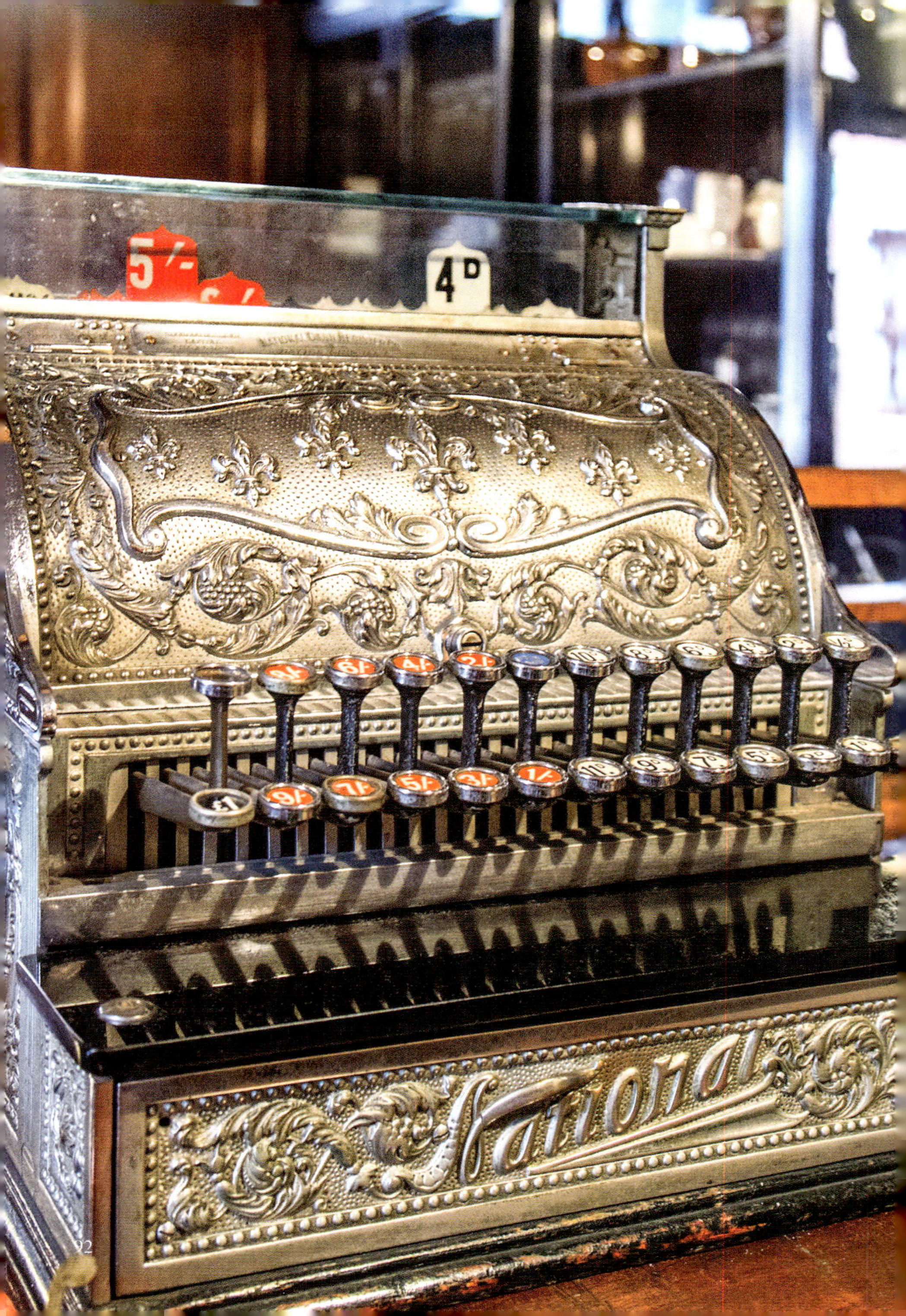
5/-
4D
National

A NATION OF SHOPKEEPERS

IT HAS OFTEN BEEN TAKEN AS AN INSULT – referring to the British as 'a nation of shopkeepers' – but in the best British tradition, our predecessors turned it into a celebration of the country's self-sufficiency and its ability to manufacture, distribute, and sell just about everything the people of an advanced industrialised society could ever want.

The phrase has often been credited to Napoleon, supposedly referring to Britain's lack of readiness for war, but there is no proof that Bonaparte ever said such a thing – and indeed why would he, as Britain seemed constantly engaged in a war, expecting a war, or re-arming after a war.

In fact, the phrase most likely comes from the writings of Adam Smith who, in his 1776 book *Wealth of Nations*, used it with pride, writing that

> 'To found a great empire for the sole purpose of raising up a people of customers, may at first sight, appear a project fit only for a nation of shopkeepers.

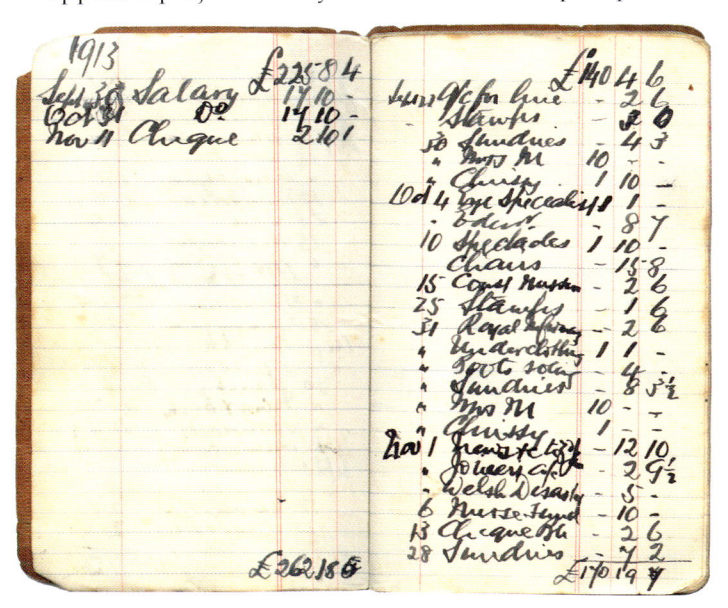

opposite page: A vintage American-built National Cash Register manufactured around 1910 and modified for British pre-decimal currency, stands on the counter of Langston's Hardware shop, part of the recreation of an early twentieth century town in the Black Country Living Museum.

below: Two pages from the household accounts book of George Masterton – the author's great grandfather – who was head teacher of a secondary school in Crossroads, Fife. In 1913 and 1914, his salary was £17.10s a month – just £210 per year. Back then, such a sum was a princely salary.

right: So popular was the picture postcard in Edwardian times that it was not unusual for shops to publish cards depicting their own premises — a clever marketing ploy. This card advertised the Brynmawr branch of the Blaina Industrial & Provident Society Ltd, one of many general stores established along 'co-operative' lines. The organisation also produced a series of postcards of their much larger 'Central Stores' in Blaina, a few miles north of Abertillery.

below: A chandler's shop, one of a number of 'typical' maritime suppliers recreated on Hartlepool's Historic Quay, now known as the National Museum of the Royal Navy Hartlepool.

It is, however, a project altogether unfit for a nation of shopkeepers, but extremely fit for a nation whose government is influenced by shopkeepers.'

By 1832, the phrase had been misquoted and misattributed so many times that the *Morning Post* sought to correct the matter in an editorial in May 1832 writing –

'This complimentary term, for so we must consider it, as applied to a Nation which has derived its principal prosperity from its commercial greatness, has been erroneously attributed, from time to time, to all the leading Revolutionists of France. To our astonishment we now find it applied exclusively to

Bonaparte. Than this nothing can be further from the fact. Napoleon was scarcely known at the time, he being merely an Officer of inferior rank, totally unconnected with politics.'

While a few luxury goods may have been imported during the nineteenth century – an increasing number of them from America – everyday objects were manufactured at home by local businesses, tailored to meet local needs.

Being 'British-made' was once a guarantee of quality, and almost all the goods offered for sale in British shops were British-made.

Indeed, until the twentieth century relatively few basic goods were imported – Britain prided herself in being relatively self-sufficient, and there were thousands of local entrepreneurs who built businesses from scratch, initially to serve local needs, but as transport infrastructure improved throughout the nineteenth century – with railways and better roads – they found their goods could be sold much more widely and even exported across Britain's growing Empire.

The nineteenth century was, however, a period which saw great changes in Britain's shopping habits.

above: A mid-Victorian ambrotype photograph on glass of a leather goods shop. Itinerant photographers travelled from town to town taking such photographs and processing them immediately in their portable darktents or caravans. They then sought to sell them to the shopkeeper.

below: Zinc baths and buckets adorn the frontage of Langston's Hardware store, one of the many shops and business premises rebuilt in the Black Country Living Museum.

right: Dating from just before the Great War, the Newcastle bakers and confectioners Tilley & Co. Ltd. commisioned coloured postcards of their shop and its wares as a marketing tool.

below: The recreation of a Victorian shopping street, complete with tramcars, at Beamish Open-Air Museum in Northumberland. Beamish is just one of several sites across the country where rescued buildings have been reassembled to give a sense of past living and shopping conditions.

When Queen Victoria came to the throne in 1837, large sheets of plate glass – introduced a decade earlier – had replaced the traditional small panes in many shop windows, as the purpose of the window changed from one of simply letting light into the interior, to being a means of enticing customers inside by displaying the shop's wares. At the same time, the majority of shops moved to a system of fixed prices, replacing the age-old tradition of barter.

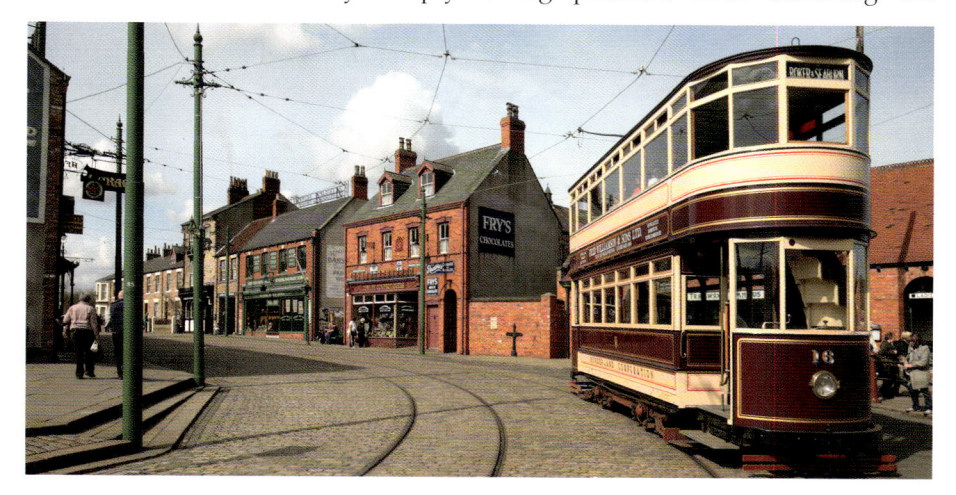

As a result, potential customers walked from one shop to another – initially to compare products and prices, but eventually simply taking pleasure from admiring the

left: The recreation of the company shop at Blaenafon Ironworks in South Wales, where the workers were issued with tokens as part of their wages, committing them to buying their provisions in the company shop — or the company's chosen shop — rather than elsewhere in the town. Some early co-operative societies even gave their cash-paying customers tokens instead of change, committing them to coming back to redeem those tokens in the shop.

below: A set of payment tokens from the Guide Post Equitable Cooperative Society near Morpeth in Northumberland. The tokens were produced by Adhill & Company of Ridge Works, Leeds.

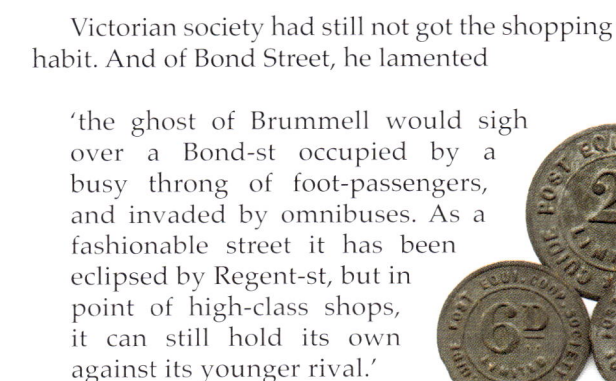

clothes, shoes or other goods on display. And so was born the idea of the 'window shopper'.

As late as 1888, Charles Dickens Jnr, in his *Dickens's Dictionary of London*, describing the appearance of London's Oxford Street, suggested that

> 'it ought to be the finest thoroughfare in the world. As a matter of fact it is not... it still contains houses which even in a third-rate street would be considered mean... although some of the handsomest and most attractive shops, even in this street of tradesmen's palaces, are on the western side, it is comparatively deserted by passengers.'

Victorian society had still not got the shopping habit. And of Bond Street, he lamented

> 'the ghost of Brummell would sigh over a Bond-st occupied by a busy throng of foot-passengers, and invaded by omnibuses. As a fashionable street it has been eclipsed by Regent-st, but in point of high-class shops, it can still hold its own against its younger rival.'

above: The American F. W. Woolworth company produced a series of Edwardian postcards of their flagship stores. In Britain they were originally known as 'F. W. Woolworth & Co. Ltd 3d & 6d Stores' and their shop at 25-25A Church Street in Liverpool was their first in the UK. It opened on 5 November 1909. They took over an existing mid-nineteenth-century Grade II listed building which is, at the time of writing, now a Clarks shoe shop.

above right: A Victorian dentist's surgery, recreated in Blists Hill.

But the only mentions he makes of shopping are likewise to be found scattered throughout his book.

There is no entry for 'shops' or 'shopping' in his gazetteer between 'shoeblacks' and 'Siam' where you might expect to find them. Shopping in Victorian London was clearly not as important as either clean shoes or knowing where the Siamese Consulate was located. But by that time, habits were changing, and within a few years, the side of the street lined with 'tradesmen's palaces' would be the busier side.

Improved public transport, and an increasingly affluent middle class in the Edwardian era, changed shopping and window-shopping into a pleasant leisure pastime.

Tram systems, first horse-drawn and later powered by steam or electricity, brought shoppers in to town centres in increasing numbers and at minimal cost.

Abandoned across the country in the 1950s, the value of trams has been recognised once again, with new tramways being introduced into many towns and cities.

During construction work for these new systems, Victorian tram lines laid into cobbled streets have briefly re-erged from under the tarmac.

A NATION OF SHOPKEEPERS

Britain's – and possibly the world's – first 'department store', Bainbridge's in Newcastle, first opened its doors in 1838 as a drapery and fashion shop. By 1859, the range of goods had expanded hugely, and the store adopted a policy of accounting by separate departments – three years before Le Bon Marche, France's claimant to be the first, did the same! From that simple operational decision came the term we all use widely today.

The Newcastle store, which has been part of the John Lewis Partnership since 1952, finally dropped the Bainbridge name in 2002 after 160 years!

By the beginning of the twentieth century, many of the store chains we know today had already made an appearance, and some were already an established presence on many high streets – Debenhams had grown from its original drapers' store in Wigmore Street, and W H Smith, established as a single newspaper stall in London in 1846, was by then present in hundreds of railway stations.

John Boot had established his eponymous chemist's shop in Nottingham in 1849, and the company had enjoyed

above: Most trams were powered by steam, or later by electricity. Neath in South Wales was unusual in opting for German-designed gas-powered trams, built in Lancaster under licence from Gasmotoren-Fabrik Deutz of Cologne. The 23 double-decker trams ran along the 4 miles between Briton Ferry and Skewen from 1875 until 1920. Tramcar No.1 survives and can be seen in Cefn Coed Colliery Museum.

left: A Victorian chemist's shop from Bournemouth, relocated to Blists Hill Victorian Town.

half a century of expansion. As the nineteenth century drew to a close, his son Jesse was in charge of a chain of more than sixty shops in over thirty towns and cities.

The modern shopping experience was very definitely up and running. Being a 'Nation of Shopkeepers' was, perhaps, not such a bad thing after all.

A number of the shops on every High Street were repairers – helping get every last ounce of wear out of everyday items. A far cry from the throwaway society of today where many young women wear an outfit only once.

The welcome sight of a dry and warm tram on a wet day at the Black Country Living Museum. Tram No.34 was built in 1919 for Wolverhampton District Tramways and could seat 32 passengers. It is one of the museum's operational fleet of three cars dating from 1909 to 1920, two trolley buses and four motor buses. The collection also includes an 1892 horse-drawn double-decker tramcar.

below: Blists Hill Victorian Town's haberdashery shop. On the counter, a sign reads 'Ladies of distinction, and their daughters, can rest assured that their dress allowance is carefully and wisely spent.' From the wide range of goods displayed, it is clear that shops like this supported the employment of hundreds, perhaps thousands, of men and women across the textile industries – hat makers, lace-makers, silk weavers and many other trades. Add to that the various shop-fitting trades which were expanding as people's expectation of the shopping experience became more sophisticated.

From my great grandfather George Masterton's accounts book from 1913 to 1919, a lot can be learned about the period. Everyday items of expenditure are meticulously noted, and the costs of some surprisingly high.

For example in the month of March 1914, he spent two shillings and sixpence on postage stamps – at a time when a letter cost one penny to post, and a postcard a ha'penny.

That's an average of one letter or two postcards per day – and even with the high currency of letter-writing in those days before the telephone became commonplace, that's quite a lot.

Clothes were made – and bought – to last in those days. Nobody would expect the schoolmaster to dress anyway other than soberly, and presumably the same was expected of his wife and daughter.

Over the period chronicled within the accounts book, George did not splash out on any unnecessary fashion items. There are only a few entries detailing his clothing purchases, and none whatsoever for clothes for either 'Mrs M.' or his daughter Chrissy – so perhaps they clothed themselves out of the £10 he handed over for household expenses out of his £17.10s (£17.50) monthly salary.

In the period 1914 to 1916, only four purchases of new clothes are recorded – two for unspecified clothing from Forsyth & Company in Edinburgh – one amounting to £5.1.6d (£5.07) in 1914 and the other for £1.10.0d two years later. In between those entries, we know he spent 4/6d (22p) on a new cap and tie, £3 for a new overcoat, and £1.7.0d (£1.35) for a new pair of boots – three shillings (15p) more than they had cost in 1913.

Over that period, of course, there are numerous bills for boot repairs, each amounting to about 3/6d (17p). Those boots would have been well and truly worn in and worn down before they were replaced. When his suit started to look a little faded by May 1919, he paid 6/6d (32p) to have it dyed – thus getting a bit more use out of it.

The very first entry in the book – in late June 1913 – records that the sum of £2.10s (£2.50) was paid to the family

George Masterton photographed in his garden. The picture he handed down of life in Crossroads schoolhouse in Fife echoes the early Edwardian, perhaps even Victorian eras. His wife, Janet, is referred to as 'Mrs M.' in each monthly entry as he recorded passing her £10 of his monthly salary to cover household expenses. She continued to be referred to as 'Mrs M.' until mid-1917, when the entry changed to 'Household'.

following pages: Many shops delivered their goods using handcarts well into the twentieth century. Here a baker's cart is being repaired in the former Horsham cartwright's shop at Amberley Museum in West Sussex.

WHEEL IN
PROGRESS
10/ FOR MUSEUM
RURAL LIFE / FARNHAM

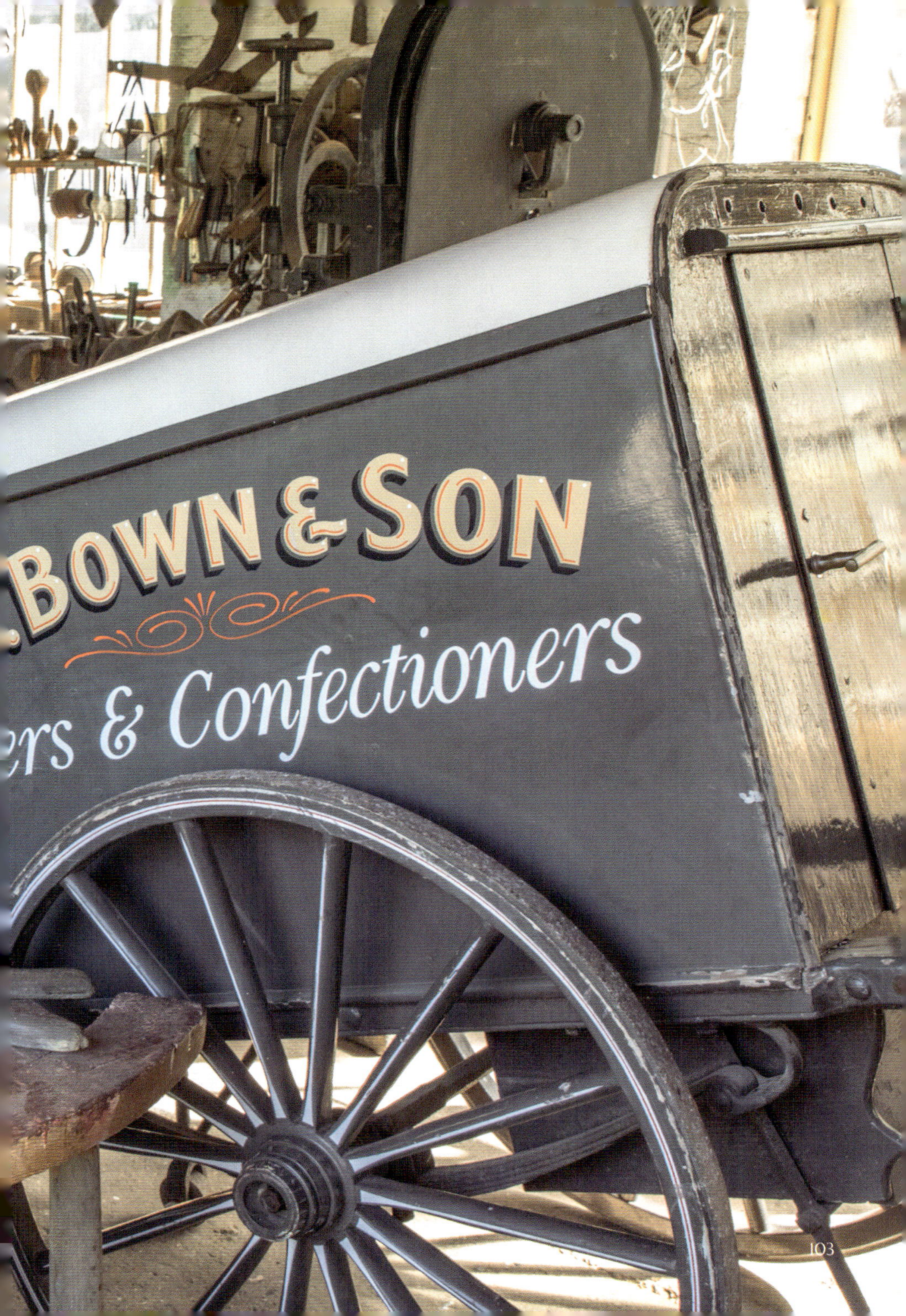
BOWN & SON
ers & Confectioners

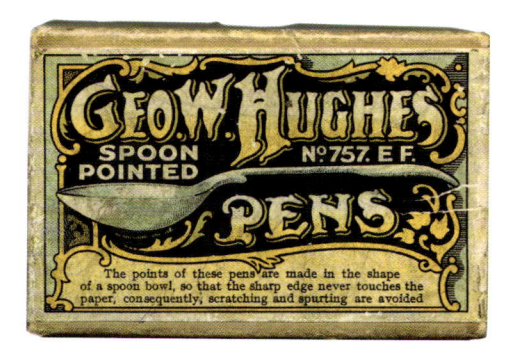

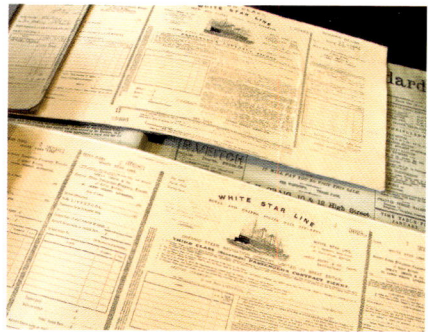

above: George W. Hughes started making pen knibs in the 1850s. In 1893 demand was such that he moved to new premises at St Pauls Penworks in Legge Lane, Birmingham. This box dates from c.1905. The firm closed in the 1960s.

top right: Planning to cross the Atlantic? White Star Line booking forms on display at Robert Smail's Print Works in Innerleithen.

middle: The preserved Bognor Regis cobbler's shop at the Amberley Museum in West Sussex.

right: S. Ockenden & Son's Ironmonger's shop, formerly at Littlehampton, also preserved at Amberley.

opposite bottom: Ceramic beer pumps at the recreated Millowners Arms in Sheffield's Kelham Island Museum.

dentist, while in the following months, rail fares for the family holiday cost a massive £3.19.6d (£3.97) – much more than the £2.4.3d (£2.21) rental for the holiday home. The following year, holiday travelling expenses exceeded £5!

A new pair of spectacles cost £1.10s (£1.50) in 1914 and £1.12.3d (£1.61) four years later, while a pair of 'eyeglasses' in the following year cost only 15 shillings (75p)! Amazingly, a second pair of glasses in 1916 cost half that – at 7/6 they were 6d cheaper than George's new umbrella!

In today's 'throwaway society' where everything is bought packed in plastic, used a few times and then discarded, the idea of such careful husbandry is almost unbelievable – but our grandparents and great-grandparents did much less damage to the planet than we are doing.

To paraphrase the words of Mr Micawber, 'Annual income two hundred and seventeen pounds, annual expenditure one hundred and seventy eight pounds sixteen and fourpence halfpenny, result happiness!'

As a schoolmaster, George Masterton and his family enjoyed a comfortable life, and well within their means. His accounts book is a fascinating record of the cost of living before and during the Great War years.

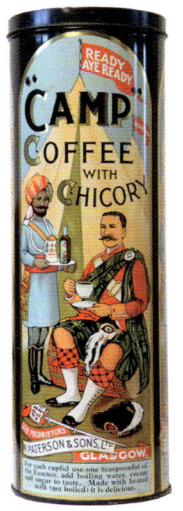

above: Camp Coffee, made in Glasgow by Paterson & Sons Ltd of Charlotte Street, was introduced in 1876 and, more than 140 years later, is still on the market. In the beginning, its label featured Sergeant-Major (later Major-General Sir) Hector Macdonald on the label, seated on a drum, being served coffee on a tray by his Sikh batman. By the 1990s, that was considered politically incorrect, and the label was redesigned (rewriting history) so that the Sikh batman and the Highlander were seated together. Macdonald, later known as 'Fighting Mac' became a military legend during the Boer War.

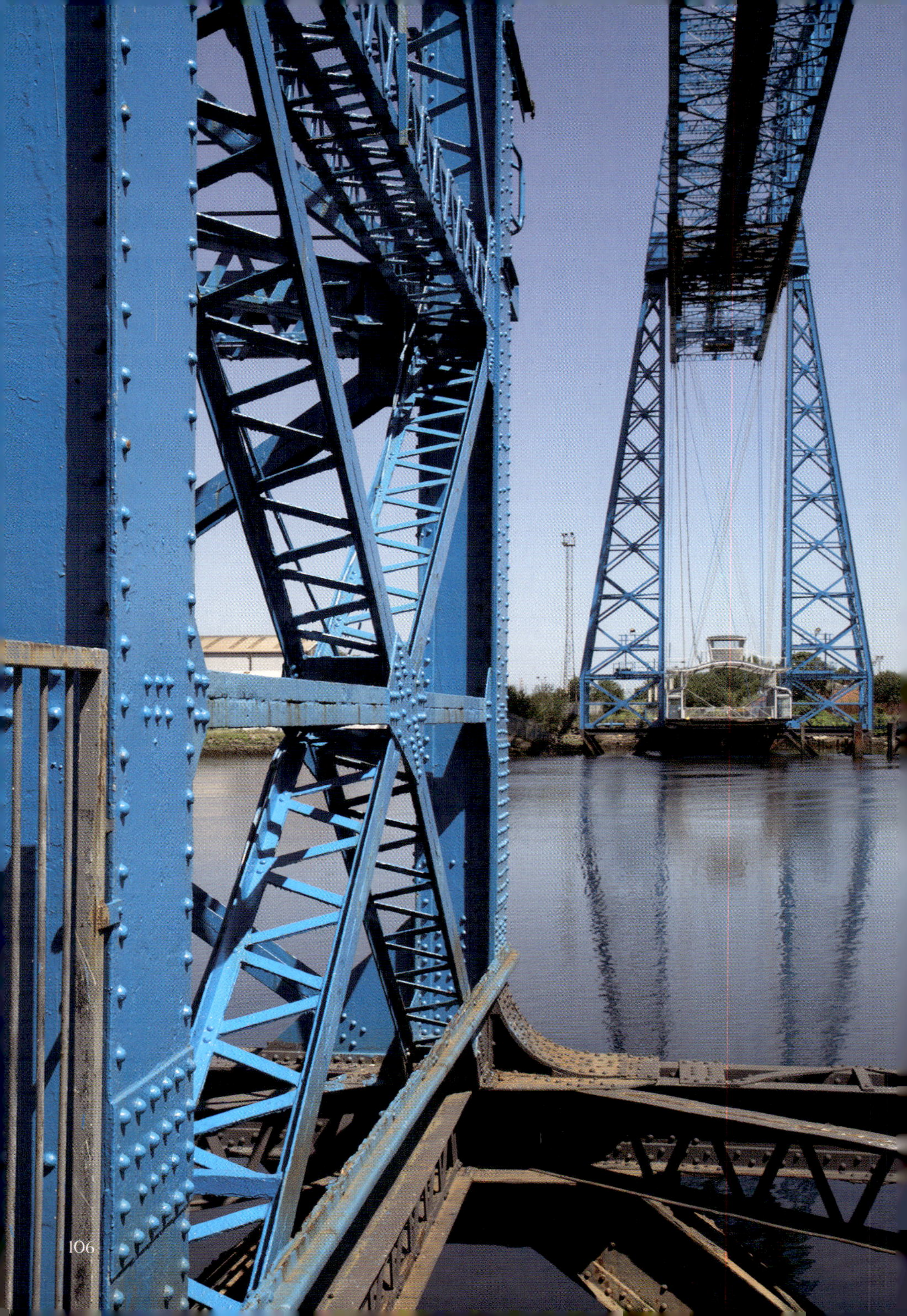

PHOTOGRAPHING THE INDUSTRIAL WORLD

THE BUILDING OF INDUSTRIAL BRITAIN was well documented by the new art of photography. Photography was invented in the late 1830s and has been improved continually from the 1840s right up to the present day.

The British inventor William Henry Fox Talbot, squire of Lacock Abbey in Wiltshire, introduced the idea of the photographic negative from which multiple prints could be made. His first successful negative – little bigger than a postage stamp – was made in August 1835.

By the early 1840s, the process had advanced to a point where it had obvious practical applications – initially portraits and views – but within a remarkably short time, the idea of using the new medium to record industrial Britain's new factories, railways and bridges had been suggested by the Scottish civil engineer Alexander Gordon (1802-1868).

In a paper – *Photography as Applicable to Engineering* – which he presented to the Institution of Civil Engineers in 1840, he suggested that the new medium would enable 'views of building work, or even of machinery when not in motion, to be taken with perfect accuracy in a very short space of time and with comparatively small expense.'

opposite: The Middlesbrough Transporter Bridge, crosses the Tees between Middlesbrough and Port Clarence and opened in 1911. It was designed by the Cleveland Bridge & Engineering Company and built by Sir William Arrol & Company. Photographed in 2017. To take this photograph a century ago, the photographer would have had to use a large tripod-mounted plate camera, and quite a long exposure.

below: The erection of one of the towers of the Middlesbrough bridge in 1910 – part of an extensive series of progress images recording its two-year construction. The metalwork for the bridge was prefabricated at Arrol's works in Glasgow before being assembled on site.

top: Fox Talbot's printing works at Reading was set up in the mid-1840s to handle the production of prints for several of his publications. Talbot is in the middle with the large wooden camera. In his day, prints were made from his paper calotype negatives by a long exposure outside to daylight.

above: An 1860s' portable darktent.

above right: The photographer had to coat each glass plate – breathing ether fumes from the chemicals – shrouded inside the yellow-walled darktent.

Such images, he believed, would provide an important source of information for future engineers, as well as creating a valuable record of the rapid evolution of the country's infrastructure. So it has proved, and thus was introduced the idea of the specialist industrial photographer.

Without photography, our knowledge of the world in which we live would be much less extensive, and books like this would be unheard of.

In the early days, the photographer had to coat his own materials – on paper or glass – with the light sensitive chemicals which made the process work, and carry large and unwieldy cameras on location. The materials were relatively insensitive to light, requiring long exposures, and yet the images they have handed down to us are of remarkable quality.

To add to the difficulties, until the early 1870s most plates had to be developed immediately after they were exposed, requiring the photographer to transport all the chemicals needed to process them on location, as well as a portable darkroom in which to process the negatives.

Large glass plates – 8"x10", 15"x12" and even larger – from which contact prints were made, preserved very fine detail – which many later 35mm cameras in the 1960s and '70s, with their tiny negatives, still often failed to match.

Glass, however, is a fragile and heavy material to transport to some of the challenging locations in which the early industrial photographer had to work.

Getting a modern high-resolution digital camera into some of the out-of-the-way positions from which the photographs in this book were taken proved challenging enough, but a Victorian photographer might have had to carry in excess of 50kg of equipment and materials on location, before having to manhandle the camera, a heavy tripod and wooden darkslides containing the glass plates to whichever viewpoint had been selected for the picture.

Edwardian photographers had it a little easier once smaller cameras and commercially manufactured films and plates became available – from the likes of Kodak, Agfa and other companies.

It would, of course, take almost a century and a half of evolution – from plates to film and from film to digital – before photographers had access to the highly sophisticated systems we now enjoy.

below left: Henry Fox Talbot's home, Lacock Abbey in Wiltshire, is now in the custodianship of the National Trust. The adjacent Fox Talbot Museum tells the story of Talbot's invention of the photographic negative, and stages regular exhibitions.

below: This window at Lacock Abbey was the subject of Talbot's first successful photographic negative, taken with a home-made camera obscura in August 1835. The original negative, little larger than a postage stamp, still survives.

top: For this late 1890s' image of miners working underground in a Wigan colliery, local photographer Thomas Taylor had to transport his large plate camera, tripod, plates and battery-powered electric lighting underground with him. Setting the scene up required the miners adopting poses which they could maintain for the duration of the long exposure – perhaps as long as half a minute – without moving. In underground coal seams known for having pockets of gas, a spark while connecting the cables to the batteries could have proved catastrophic. Photographed in black and white on a large glass plate, the colouring was added during the lithographic postcard printing process c.1904.

right: This photograph of the recreation of a mining gallery underground at the 'Big Pit' Welsh Mining Museum near Blaenafon was taken hand-held with a modern digital single lens reflex camera in a fraction of a second using only the low level electric lighting in the tunnel.

Today's photographer travels light, using cameras which can operate under extremely low light levels and yet deliver high quality detailed images under conditions which could never have been imagined as recently as a generation ago.

Indeed, during my own early years as a working professional photographer, Kodak High Speed Ektachrome introduced in 1960, had an ISO of only 160, a far cry from the ISO 32,000 or more at which many modern DSLRs can deliver usable images.

The industrial world responded very quickly in recognising the potential value of photography – both as

PHOTOGRAPHING THE INDUSTRIAL WORLD

left`: One of James Mudd's photographs for Beyer-Peacock — a new locomotive for Swedish Railways, 1856.

below: A London & South Western Railway L14 class 4-6-0, photographed in matt grey primer at Nine Elms, 1907.

bottom: SR Mogul No.31806 heads a train into Corfe Castle Station on the Swanage Railway in 2018.

a means of keeping a visual record and as an aid to promoting the sales of its products within a wider marketplace.

An early adopter of photography in the mid-1850s was the Beyer-Peacock company in Manchester, then one of the world's largest manufacturers of steam locomotives. Enlisting the services of local photographer James Mudd, they pioneered – and maintained – a policy of having the first of each new locomotive design photographed as it left their workshops in Gorton.

Mudd initially used the slow but highly detailed Waxed Paper process, invented in France by Gustave le Gray, producing 15"x12" paper negatives, many of which still survive and are now part of the collection in Manchester's Museum of Science & Industry.

With the locomotives outdoors in the company's yard, the long exposures were not a problem.

111

When the photographs became more important as marketing tools, the locomotives were specially painted in a matt grey primer to minimise reflections.

In the late 1850s, Isambard Kingdom Brunel was equally certain of the potential value of photography – especially as he was in poor health at the time his great steamship, the SS *Great Eastern* was being built on the Thames.

As he could not regularly visit the shipyard, he commissioned one of photography's rising stars – Robert Howlett – to take pictures throughout the build On one occasion, with Brunel on

above: Brunel's *Great Eastern* under construction on the Thames, 1857, photographed by Robert Howlett with a large format wet collodion glass plate camera on a temporary tower.

right: Shipbuilding on the Clyde, 2017 – Caledonian MacBrayne's new ferry MV *Glen Sannox* under construction as Hull 801 at the Ferguson Marine shipyard in Port Glasgow, photographed with a modern DSLR from the top of a cherry-picker. The ferry will operate services to Arran.

PHOTOGRAPHING THE INDUSTRIAL WORLD

left: Brunel's first iron-hulled steamship, the SS *Great Britain* was rescued from the Falkland Islands, returned to the UK, and restored over a period of decades to something like her original appearance.

below: The SS *Great Britain* tied up in Cumberland Basin, Bristol, in 1844. This photograph, long attributed to Henry Fox Talbot, is now thought to have been taken by his friend the Reverend Calvert Richard Jones. It is believed to be the first photograph ever taken of a steamship.

site, Howlett also took the iconic portrait of him with his stovepipe hat, standing in front of the ship's launching chains.

Howlett's images survive today in several public and private collections as remarkable examples of the medium.

Only one early photograph is known to survive of Brunel's earlier iron ship, the SS *Great Britain* – now restored back in the Bristol dry dock where she was built – and that was taken on a calotype paper negative. The SS *Great Eastern*, of course, survived for many years and was regularly photographed in both Britain and the USA.

113

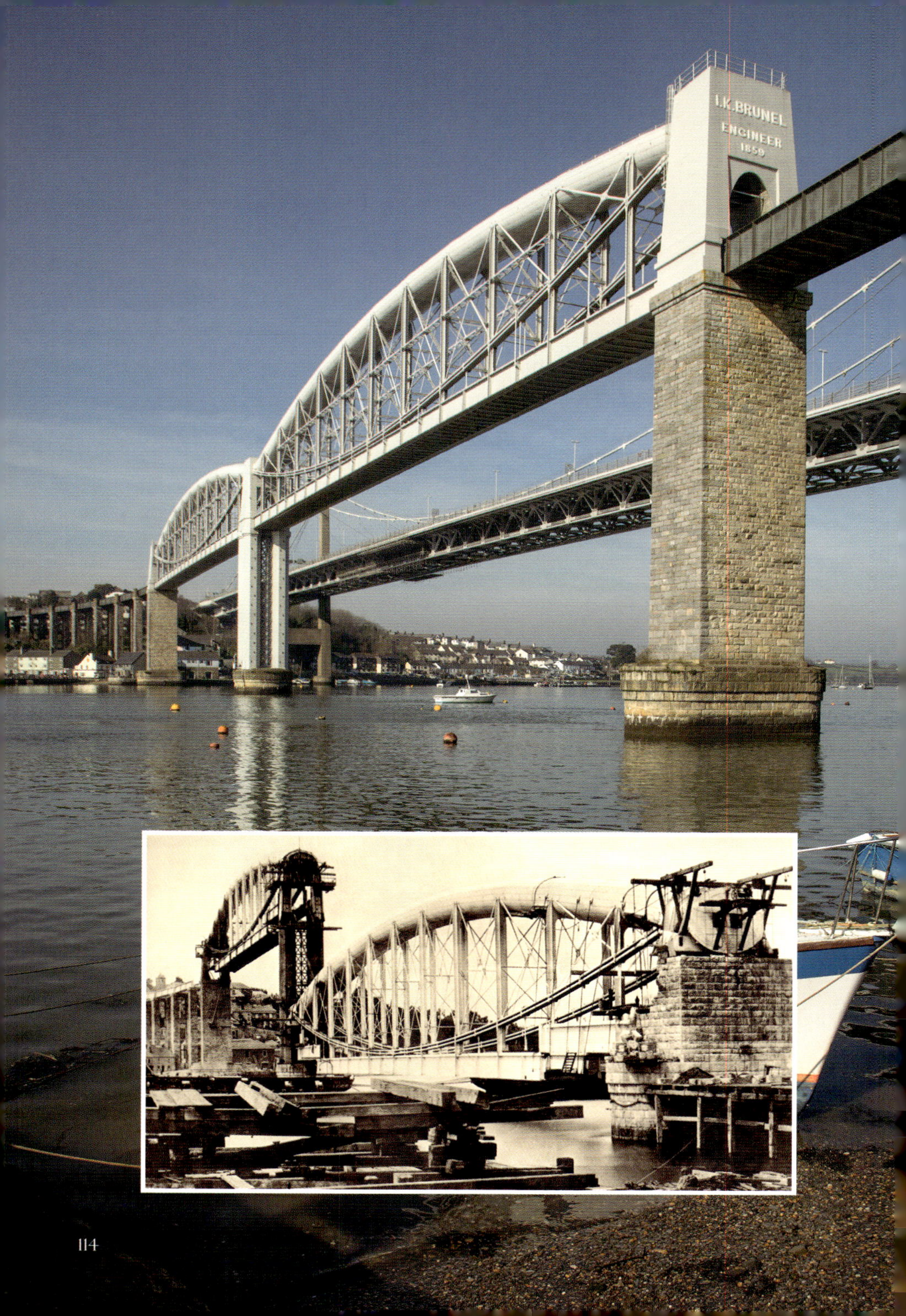
I.K.BRUNEL
ENGINEER
1859

PHOTOGRAPHING THE INDUSTRIAL WORLD

Along with photographing the construction of Brunel's Saltash Bridge over the River Tamar between Devon and Cornwall, the *Great Eastern* was to be one of Howlett's last commissions as he died in 1858 at the age of only twenty-seven.

His remarkable pictures constitute one of the earliest records to be made of a ship under construction, establishing a tradition which has been maintained now for more than a century and a half.

Another engineer who saw the value of 'progress photography' was the bridge and railway builder Charles Blacker Vignoles, whose mammoth engineering projects took him all over the world.

To take progress pictures of his commission in the late 1840s, to build the first permanent bridge over the River Dnieiper, or Dnipro, at Kiev, he picked two of the finest photographers of his time – Roger Fenton who would later achieve widespread fame as the photographer of the Crimean War, and John Cooke Bourne, a railway illustrator.

An entry from Vignoles' diaries, dated 16 October 1848, recounts the start of the photographic work

> 'explained to Mr. Bourne the views I wanted taken from the mound in the garden – where in clear weather the [temporary] Bridge could be seen – the works of the dams and the temporary bridge and Schweitzer's Colony being very plain.'

opposite page: Isambard Kingdom Brunel's single-track Royal Albert Bridge which links Devon and Cornwall over the River Tamar, seen from the Devon shore. It was opened in 1859 and is a 'lenticular truss' bridge, giving all the strength and stability of a suspension bridge but without the need for tall towers and anchored cables. Its innovative design is in sharp contrast to the cost-saving design of the other bridges and viaducts which punctuated Brunel's broad-gauge line from Plymouth to Truro.

inset: The bridge under construction. Each truss was built on the shore and floated out into the river before being raised into position by hydraulic jacks as the tower was built beneath it.

left: John Cooke Bourne photographed the construction of the Dneiper bridge every week, sending images back from Kiev to Vignoles. This view, taken on a paper negative, shows the wooden decking being laid and was photographed in early 1853, just a few weeks before the bridge was opened to traffic.

right: The north-east cantilever bedplate for the Forth railway bridge under construction in July 1886 — a detail from one of Evelyn Carey's photographs. At that time over 3000 people were working on the bridge.

below: The scale of the Forth Bridge dwarfs a train crossing in this view taken from North Queensferry.

The 'Schweitzer's Colony' was the workmen's camp, and that date marked the start of the Bourne's five year project. He was the lead photographer on the project right up until the bridge opened in 1853, with Fenton's involvement being limited to taking stereoscopic (3D) views. Surprisingly, for a project which was photographed almost every week during construction, very few pictures survive. Perhaps part of the reason for that is that Vignoles and Fenton fell out before the project was completed, with Vignoles actually threatening court action if Fenton did not hand over the negatives.

And as for Bourne, well it was not until 1858 that Vignoles finally got round to paying his final invoice for services completed four years earlier, and as far as can be ascertained, he never undertook another photographic assignment, despite having designed and patented a new professional camera in 1855.

Alexander Gordon, the visionary who first suggested applying photography to engineering back in 1840, was still alive when the largest bridge construction project ever announced in Scotland – the building of a railway bridge across the Firth of Forth between North and South Queensferry – was proposed in 1864. However he did not live to see work start on Thomas Bouch's design – a three-tower suspension

above: James Valentine of Dundee also photographed the bridge regularly throughout construction. This view was taken in August 1887.

left: The view from a boat sailing under the Forth Bridge on the way to Inchcolm Island. The sheer complexity of its construction is a spectacular reminder of the vision of Victorian engineers.

The Great Gantry, Harland & Wolff's, Shipyard, Belfast

The World's Greatest Gantry, in Harland and Wolff's North Shipyard, Belfast.

above: The 6000 ton Arrol Gantry at Harland & Wolff's Belfast shipyard was a massive structure. It became the subject of many popular postcards. Erected in 1908, it measured 840ft long, 240ft wide, and 228ft high. It was demolished in the 1960s.

right: The hulls of the White Star Line's RMS *Titanic* and RMS *Olympic* under construction in the Arrol Gantry at Harland & Wolff.

bridge – which was abandoned after the collapse of Bouch's Tay bridge in 1879. Some photographs of preliminary work were taken, and the base of one of the towers was built. It still stands today, carrying a small warning beacon.

It would be nearly twenty years before the idea was resurrected – by which time Bouch was disgraced, and the cantilevered design by Consulting Engineers John Fowler and Benjamin Baker which we know today was commissioned.

It would be constructed by Scotland's 'Man of Steel', Sir William Arroll.

Perhaps Fowler and Baker's design was over-engineered – the Tay Bridge disaster was still fresh in the public mind – but it is now hard to imagine the Firth without that iconic structure.

Baker and Fowler saw huge benefits in using photography, employing Evelyn George Carey to record the project at every stage during the seven years it took to complete.

His eye for engineering detail makes many of his images especially interesting, showing aspects of the early stages of the bridge's structure which are no longer visible.

Interestingly, Carey had been trained, not as a photographer, but as an engineer, initially developing a passion for photography as a hobby. Thus, while hired as an engineer, his brief was to use both his engineering knowledge and his skills with a large format camera to photograph every aspect of its construction.

above left: The gearing from the waterwheel to the mill machinery at Quendale Mill in the Shetland Islands. Photography in conditions like this only became possible with small hand-held cameras.

above: One of the beam engines at Crofton Pumping Station on the Kennet & Avon Canal in Wiltshire.

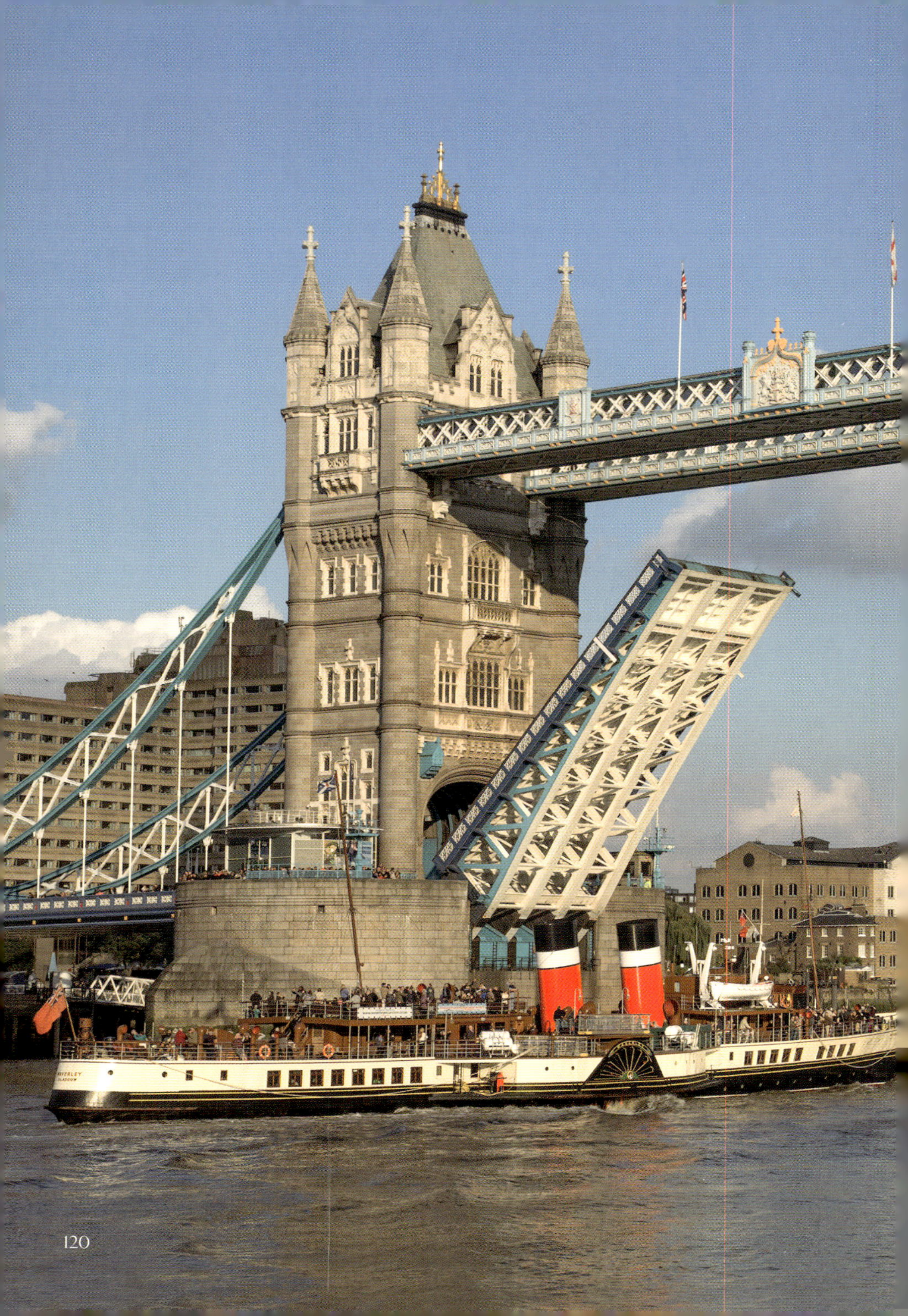

PHOTOGRAPHING THE INDUSTRIAL WORLD

The Forth Bridge is unique and world famous. Now 130 years old and still in constant use, it was enrolled by UNESCO as a World Heritage Site in 2015.

For thirty years following the bridge's opening, Carey worked for Sir William Arrol & Company, the Glasgow-based engineers who would go on to build many other iconic structures, amongst them the replacement Tay Bridge, London's Tower Bridge, the Tees Transporter Bridge in Middlesbrough and the huge Arrol Gantry at Harland & Wolff's Belfast shipyard where the RMS *Titanic* and RMS *Olympic* were both built.

All of those projects would be extensively photographed during their construction, both by 'official' photographers and by professional studios recognising the commercial value of such images – for example, the construction of the Tay and Forth railway bridges were both the subjects of extensive series of published images by Dundee professional James Valentine. Some of the photographs of the Tay Bridge disaster were even re-published as picture postcards a quarter of a century after the bridge collapsed.

By the time construction work on the Forth Bridge started in 1882, the sensitivity of photographic plates had increased

opposite: The 1947-built paddle steamer *Waverley* – one of the most iconic steamships in the world – passing under London's equally iconic Tower Bridge, the steel internal skeleton of which was built by Arrol.

below: Two 1893 views of Tower Bridge under construction. Every stage of the seven-year construction of the bridge was photographed, from 1887 until 1894.

122

considerably and exposure times had become shorter, allowing much more animated industrial scenes to be captured – often with the workers posed carefully with something to lean against or hold on to.

Even though shorter exposures had long been possible with smaller cameras, it was not uncommon, right up until the late nineteenth century, for them to have to hold their positions for several minutes, as the photographer would use a very small lens aperture to get maximum sharpness, and that in turn required long exposures.

For engineering purposes, large plates were considered essential to give the fine technical detail which industrial customers needed. Such images were rarely enlarged, so if a large print was needed, a large negative was essential.

Cameras taking glass plates of 16" x 12" and larger were not unusual in the nineteenth century, while sheets of film up to 10"x8" in size remained popular with industrial photographers well into the second half of the twentieth century.

When one considers the challenge of getting large and very heavy cameras and glass plates into almost inaccessible places – such as on the scaffolding above Tower Bridge, for example – the skill and tenacity of the photographers who took these amazing pictures have to be marvelled at.

Getting a hand-held rollfilm camera out on to the jib of a dockside crane in Manchester Docks on a freezing February morning in the late 1960s was challenge enough for me.

Today the in-house industrial photographic department is a thing of the past, driven out of business by increasing running costs and a much less formal expectation of the sort of photography which is needed to market industrial products. Large cameras and long exposures generally meant that few people appeared in early industrial images. Now, at least, our pictures are usually populated.

opposite: The world's first Giant Cantilever Crane, 150 feet tall and able to lift 200 tons, built in 1907 by Sir William Arrol, now stands alone at the former John Brown's Clydebank shipyard.

inset left: Looking down from the jib

inset right: Inside the winch-house which sits on the rear end of the jib.

above: A postcard of North Eastern Marine Engineering's 1909 crane, now demolished, which despite the claim to be the biggest in the world, was the same height as the John Brown yard's crane.

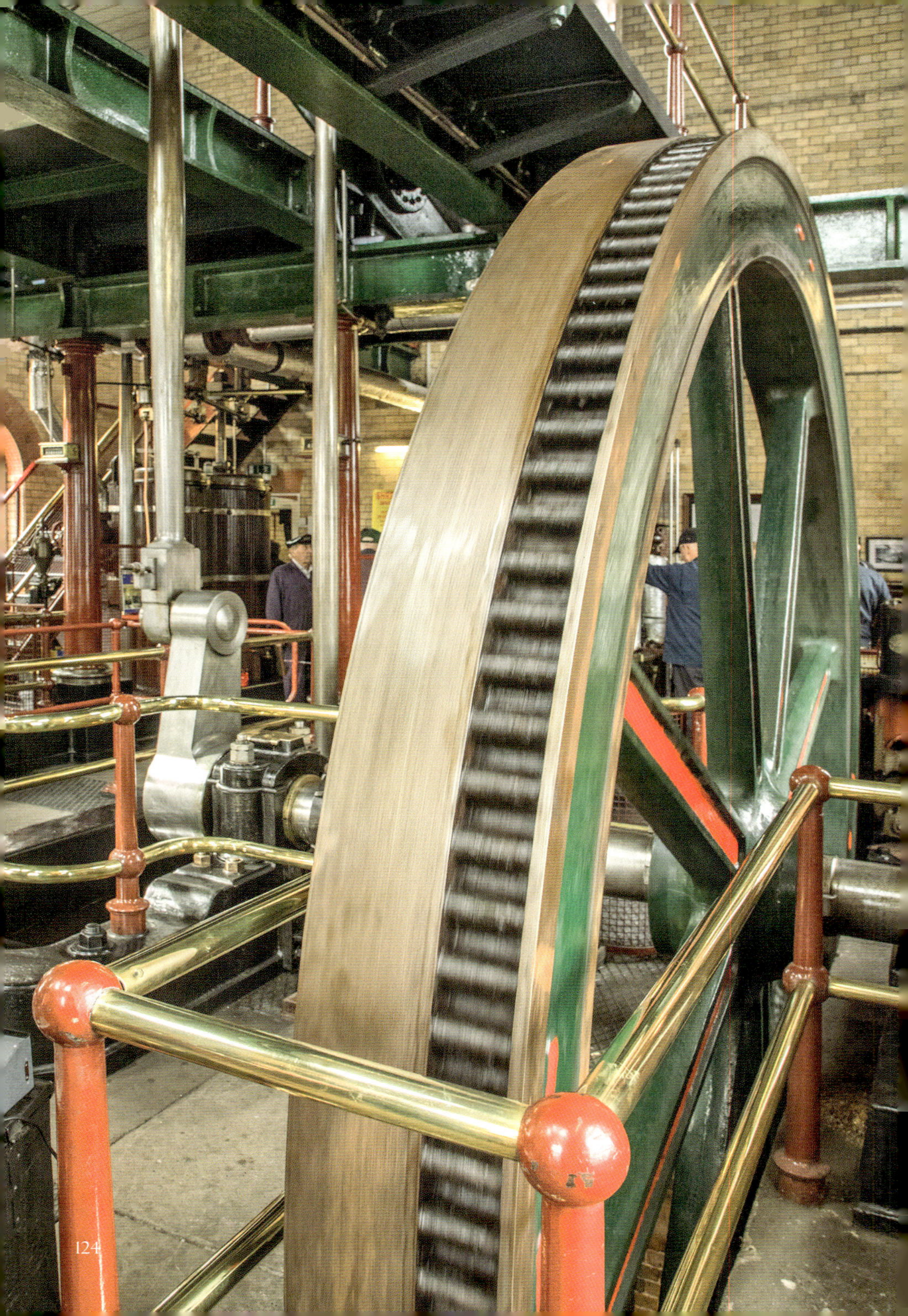

GAZETTEER
PREFACE AND INTRODUCTION

Brede Steam Giants
www.bredesteamgiants.co.uk tel: 01323 897310
Waterworks Lane, Brede, East Sussex, TN31 6HG
Hastings Waterworks' giant Worthington Simpson and Tangye triple-expansion pumping engines are currently run on compressed air until a new boiler can be funded, on the first Sunday of the month and Bank Holiday Mondays. One of the original two 410hp Tangye engines survives, the other having been removed in 1969. The 420hp Worthington Simpson engine was installed new in 1940 to meet a need for additional pumping capacity. Other engines, rescued from sites in the area, have been brought to the waterworks.

Bursledon Windmill
www.hampshireculture.org.uk/bursledon-windmill tel: 023 8040 4999
Windmill Lane, Southampton SO31 8BG
Built in 1814, it served the local community for more than seventy years before falling into disrepair. Now back in working order, the last working windmill in Hampshire is open 10am – 4pm Saturdays and Sundays, March to October.

Cefn Coed Colliery Museum
www.cwmdulais.org.uk/cefncoed tel: 01639-750556
Crynant, Neath SA10 8SN
Home to the largest horizontal duplex winding engine still working in Wales, albeit now turned by electricity rather than steam. Cefn Coed was the deepest anthracite mine in the world and thus required a powerful engine.

Coleham Pumping Station
www.colehampumpingstation.co.uk tel: 01743 281205
Longden Coleham, Shrewsbury, Shropshire SY3 7DN
The pumping station's pair of Woolf double-acting rotative beam engines (*left*) were built by W. R. Renshaw of Stoke-on-Trent in 1899 and could raise 1.2 million gallons of water daily. The engines are steamed on specific Saturdays and Sundays from March to October – check website for details.

Kelham Island Museum
www.simt.co.uk/kelham-island-museum/iron-and-steel-collection
tel: 0114 272 2106   Alma Street, Sheffield S3 8RY
Explores the history of steelmaking, its origins, the inventions, the workers, the products, from Benjamin Huntsman's invention of crucible steel in

1742, to Bessemer's mass production method in 1856, and Harry Brearley's discovery of stainless steel in 1913. On display is one of the last 25 ton converters in the world, used by British Steel at Workington until 1974. Star attraction, however, is seeing the massive River Don Engine in steam.

Museum of Science & Industry Manchester
www.mosi.org.uk tel: 0161 832 2244
Liverpool Road, Castlefield, Manchester M3 4FP
Housed in five listed buildings including Liverpool Road Station, the world's first passenger station, the museum covers a wide range of themes focusing on Manchester's contribution to science and industry. The six sections of the Revolution Manchester gallery explore Transport Revolutions, Computer Age, Engineering, Energy, Cottonopolis and the Structure of Matter.

National Coal Mining Museum for England
www.ncm.org.uk tel: 01924 848806
Caphouse Colliery, Overton, Wakefield WF4 4RH
Extensive restored pit and museum on the 17 acre site of Hope Pit. Includes 1876 steam winding engine. Underground tours 130m below ground. Extensive exhibitions of memorabilia and photographs in the former miners' baths. Free admission.

National Slate Museum
www.museumwales.ac.uk/slate tel: 0300 111 2333
Llanberis, Gwynedd LL55 4TY
Set in the Victorian workshops of Dinorwig Quarry which closed in 1969, the museum tells the story of Welsh slate against the dramatic backdrop of Elidir Mountain and its centuries of slate workings. Regular demonstrations of slate dressing and slate carving. The workshops, buildings and surrounding landscape are set out as if workmen have just put down their tools and left for home. Open daily (except Saturdays in winter). Admission free.

New Lanark
www.newlanark.org tel: 01555 661345
New Lanark, South Lanarkshire ML11 9DB
Five-storey cotton mill, built 1784. Originally founded in 1786 by David Dale, the mill and its community rose to world fame under the guidance of Robert Owen. Now restored and listed as a World Heritage Site, by 1799 New Lanark was the biggest cotton mill in Scotland and one of the largest industrial complexes in the world. At its peak, over 2000 people lived or worked in the village, and the mill continued manufacturing until 1968.

Quarry Bank Mill, Styal
www.nationaltrust.org.uk/quarry-bank tel: 01625 527468
Styal, Wilmslow, Cheshire SK9 4LA
While primarily preserved as a water-powered cotton mill, Quarry Bank now has two working steam engines similar to those which it operated in the past – one is a rotative beam engine (maker unknown) from the 1830s and used at Challinor's Sawmills in Macclesfield until 1912, the other a single cylinder horizontal engine, maker also unknown, rescued from Jesse Street Dyeworks in Bradford and restored. It is thought to be by William Bradley of Gooder Lane Ironworks, Brighouse. Admission charge.

Quendale Mill, Shetland
www.quendalemill.co.uk tel: 01950 460969
Dunrossness, Shetland ZE2 9JD
The beautifully restored mill is now managed by the South Mainland Community History Group. The water-powered mill was built in 1867 and began milling grain the following year, continuing until the mill shut down in 1948. In addition to the mill itself, there are displays of agricultural machinery, and temporary exhibitions on a range of topics. Open daily mid-April to mid-October. Admission charge.

Stanley Mills
www.historic-scotland.gov.uk tel: 01738 828268
Stanley, Perthshire PH1 4QE
Built in 1786 by a hairpin bend in the River Tay, where tremendous water-power was available, the mill's machinery was initially powered by water wheels, later by electricity generated by water turbines. The cotton mill was built by local merchants, with support from Richard Arkwright, and remains the finest example of an Arkwright mill. Now in the care of Historic Scotland. Very little machinery is preserved, but the recorded voices of former workers echo through the empty mill floors. The Bell Mill is one of the oldest surviving in the world.

Tower Bridge Exhibition
www.towerbridge.org.uk tel: 020 7403 3761
Tower Bridge Road, London SE1 2UP
A chance to explore the iconic bridge and walk across the glass walkway on the upper level. The exhibition describing how the bridge was built can be found in the south tower and along the upper walkway. Also open are the Victorian engine rooms below the road on the north side of the river, the engines beautifully restored. Open daily. Admission charge.

Westonzoyland Pumping Station
www.wzlet.org tel: 01278 691595
Hoopers Lane, Westonzoyland, Bridgwater TA7 0LS
The Museum of Steam Power and Land Drainage celebrates the role of steam – and later power sources – in draining the Somerset Levels. Star attraction is the 1861 Easton & Amos patent two-cylinder vertical condensing engine which drove the station's centrifugal pump for ninety years until 1951 and is now regularly run on steaming days. More than 30 engines have been rescued from local factories and mills, making the collection one of the largest in the UK.

Wilton Windmill
www.wiltonwindmill.co.uk tel: 01672 870266
Wilton, Great Bedwyn near Marlborough SN8 3SW
The only working windmill in Wessex, Wilton Windmill was built in 1821 and was in use for over a century, before being abandoned. Fully restored and returned to service in 1976, it is open for tours 2pm-5pm Sundays and Bank Holiday Mondays, Easter and the end of September.

ABOUT TIME

The Clockmakers' Museum
www.sciencemuseum.org.uk/see-and-do/clockmakers-museum
tel: 020 7998 8120
Science Museum, Exhibition Road, South Kensington, London SW7 2DD
The Worshipful Company of Clockmakers' collection, now in the Science Museum, traces the story of London's clockmakers. The collection includes 1000 watches, 80 clocks, 25 marine chronometers, a number of sundials, and one of John Harrison's early chronometers. Admission free.

Leeds City Museum
www.museumsandgalleries.leeds.gov.uk tel: 0113 378 5001
Millennium Square, Leeds LS2 8BH
The only museum outside London to have a permanent display about John Harrison, together with one of his earliest clocks.

Museum of Timekeeping
www.museumoftimekeeping.org.uk tel: 01636 817 601
British Horological Institute, Upton Hall, Upton, Notts NG23 5TE
Exhibits include the watch worn by Captain Scott on his polar expedition of 1912 and the first Speaking Clock. Open Fridays 11am – 3pm, April to Sept.

Royal Museums Greenwich
www.rmg.co.uk tel: 020 8312 6608
Blackheath Avenue, Greenwich SE10 8XJ
The Royal Observatory Greenwich holds some of history's most iconic timepieces and tells the stories of John Harrison's groundbreaking marine chronometer H1, Charles Shepherd's 'master clock', and the famous Greenwich Time Ball.

Verdant Works, Dundee
www.verdantworks.com tel: 01382 309060
W. Henderson's Wynd, Dundee DD1 5BT
The Verdant Works is the only working jute museum in the United Kingdom, and is housed in a former jute mill. The museum tells the story of jute production in Dundee – once so important that the city was known as 'Juteopolis'. Try 'clocking in' as you enter the premises. Regular demonstrations of jute weaving on historic looms take place.

World Museum, Liverpool / National Museums, Liverpool
www.liverpoolmuseums.org.uk/wml/collections/horology
tel: 0151 478 4393
William Brown Street, Liverpool L3 8EN
The collection includes 1200 timepieces including some of Liverpool's earliest watches by Samuel and Thomas Aspinwall, an astronomical regulator clock by William Bond, observatory clocks and regulators, turret clocks, chronometers, precision watches and special industrial clocks and watches.

THE RISE AND DEMISE OF THE MILL

Bolton Steam Museum
www.nmes.org tel: 01204 846490
Mornington Road, Bolton BL1 4EU
Home to the Northern Mill Engine Society Collection, Bolton Steam Museum is housed in a large former warehouse at the Musgrave Spinning Company's Atlas Mills – once one of the largest spinning complexes in the country. The collection has grown steadily over the past fifty years and now comprises more than 30 engines. There are five steaming weekends each year, but the engines can be viewed, some turned by electricity, every Wednesday and Sunday – check website for dates and details. Admission free, but donations appreciated.

Coldharbour Mill
www.coldharbourmill.org.uk tel: 01884 840960
Coldharbour, Uffculme, Devon EX15 3EE
A spinning mill built by Thomas Fox to spin woollen and later worsted yarns in 1799, the mill is a rare survival of Georgian architecture and industry. Since reopening as a museum in 1982 the mill still produces worsted yarns and cloths on its period machinery, powered by an 1821 breast shot water wheel. An 1867 Kittoe & Brotherhood Beam Engine and a 1910 Pollitt & Wigzell 300hp Steam Engine are still regularly operated on 'steam days'.

Hall I'th Wood, Bolton
www.boltonlams.co.uk › hall-i-th-wood-museum tel: 01204 332377
Green Way, Crompton Way, Bolton BL1 8UA
An early sixteenth-century timbered property which, in the late eighteenth century was part let to Samuel Crompton, and it was there that he built the first spinning mule, a milestone in the mechanisation of spinning. Open Tuesday 10-4 and Saturday 12-4 only.

Helmshore Mills Textile Museum
www.lancashire.gov.uk/leisure-and-culture/museums/helmshore-mills-textile-museum tel: 01706 226459
Holcombe Road, Helmshore, Rossendale BB4 4NP
Two original Lancashire textile mills, Higher Mill and Whitaker's Mill, are together known as Helmshore Mills Textile Museum. Higher Mill contains a large waterwheel with five pairs of fulling stocks, while Whitakers Mill houses a unique collection of industrial machinery. Open Friday-Sunday 12 til 4, April to October.

Knockando Woolmill
www.kwc.co.uk tel: 01256 892065
Knockando, Aberlour AB38 7RP
This restored mill in the heart of Speyside has been manufacturing woollen textiles on the banks of the Knockando Burn since at least 1784 and is the oldest continually operating rural mill in the country. It still contains a range of working Victorian equipment while, alongside in a new building, modern equipment is being used to weave some beautiful fabrics. Free admission, donations welcome, and an excellent café.

Masson Mills
www.massonmills.co.uk tel: 01629 581001
Derby Rd, Matlock Bath, Derbyshire DE4 3PY
Sir Richard Arkwright's vast 1783 Masson Mills are the finest surviving and best preserved example of an Arkwright cotton mill. Working textile museum illustrating Arkwright's legacy. Collection of historic textile machinery dating from the eighteenth-twentieth centuries. Working machinery demonstrations daily. Open January-November, closed December.

New Lanark
www.newlanark.org tel: 01555 661345
New Lanark, South Lanarkshire ML11 9DB
Five-storey cotton mill and extensive workers' housing, established by the banks of the Clyde in 1786. Originally founded by David Dale, the mill and its community rose to world fame under the guidance of Robert Owen. Now restored and listed as a UNESCO World Heritage Site, by 1799 New Lanark was the biggest cotton mill in Scotland and one of the largest industrial complexes in the world, employing over 2000 people. The restored workers' houses, the school and other facilities are all open to the public. Surprisingly, the mules are now used to spin wool rather than cotton.

Paradise Mill & Macclesfield Silk Museum
www.silkmacclesfield.org.uk/museums/paradise-mill tel: 01625 423883
Park Lane, Macclesfield, Cheshire SK11 6TJ
Paradise Mill is the centrepiece of Macclesfield's Silk Museum, where visitors can experience the weaving floor of a working handloom silk mill, one of the last to close in the town. The original machinery is still operated by expert guides. In the Silk Museum itself, the story of Macclesfield silk is told through displays and restored machinery. Museum open Mon-Sat, mill tours daily at 11.45, 13.00 and 14.15.

Quarry Bank Mill, Styal
www.nationaltrust.org.uk/quarry-bank tel: 01625 527468
Styal, Wilmslow, Cheshire SK9 4LA
While primarily preserved as a water-powered cotton mill, Quarry Bank now has two working steam engines similar to those which it operated in the past – one is a rotative beam engine (maker unknown) from the 1830s and used at Challinor's Sawmills in Macclesfield until 1912, the other a single cylinder horizontal engine, maker also unknown, rescued from Jesse Street Dyeworks in Bradford and restored. It is thought to be by William Bradley of Gooder Lane Ironworks, Brighouse.

Queen Street Mill, Burnley
www.lancashire.gov.uk/acs/sites/museums/qsm tel: 01282 412 555 Queen Street , Harle Syke, Burnley, Lancashire BB10 2HX
The Grade 1 listed building – built between 1894 and 1895 – is the last working 19th century steam powered weaving mill in the country. The 500hp tandem steam engine, 'Peace' – built by William Roberts of Nelson – complete with its Lancashire boiler, still drives the 308 looms from 1894 in the weaving shed. The looms, which are the mill's originals, were built by Pemberton & Company of Burnley and Harling & Todd also of Burnley.

Stanley Mills
www.historic-scotland.gov.uk tel: 01738 828268
Stanley, Perthshire PH1 4QE
Built in 1786, the mill's machinery was initially powered by water wheels, later by electricity generated by water turbines. The cotton mill was built by local merchants, with support from Richard Arkwright, and is the finest surviving example of an Arkwright mill. Little machinery is preserved, but the recorded voices of former workers echo through the empty mill floors.

Stott Park Bobbin Mill
www.english-heritage.org.uk/daysout/properties/stott-park-bobbin-mill tel: 0870 333 1181   Colton, Ulverston, Cumbria LA12 8AX
Working bobbin mill, built in 1835 by John Harrison and now restored to working order by English Heritage, Stott Park is typical of hundreds of small bobbin mills which used locally coppiced wood to turn out bobbins for the cotton industry. The horizontal steam engine which drove the mill was built by William Bradley at Gooder Lane Ironworks in Brighouse, and is now steamed on the first weekend of every month, and on Bank Holidays.

Strutt's North Mill, Belper
www.belpernorthmill.org tel: 01773 880474
Bridgefoot, Belper, Derbyshire DE56 1YD
The 1804 North Mill, originally water-powered, is part of the Derwent Valley Mills World Heritage Site and tells the story of cotton spinning and stocking making, and how Belper became the world's first factory community. Working historic machinery captures the atmosphere of a Victorian cotton mill and includes 80 spinning frames, 136 carding engines.16 drawing frames and four stretching frames.

Verdant Jute Works, Dundee
www.verdantworks.com tel: 01382 309060
W. Henderson's Wynd, Dundee DD1 5BT
The Verdant Works is the only working jute museum in the United Kingdom, and is housed in a former jute mill. The museum tells the story of jute production in Dundee – once so important that the city was known as 'Juteopolis'. Displays include an early James Watt rotative beam engine with William Murdoch's 'sun and planet' gears. Regular demonstrations of jute weaving on historic looms.

Whitchurch Silk Mill
www.whitchurchsilkmill.org.uk tel: 01256 892065
28 Winchester Street, Whitchurch, Hampshire RG28 7AL
The mill has been producing silk since 1817, when it was bought and converted by a silk weaver from Spitalfields, and it is now the oldest silk mill in Britain still in its original building. The Georgian mill – the current waterwheel dates from the 1860s – still weaves silk using nineteenth-century machinery. Until the 1890s, when power looms were installed, all silks were woven on handlooms. Open Tuesday to Sunday, admission charge.

SICKLES, NEEDLES AND NAILS

Abbeydale Industrial Hamlet
www.simt.co.uk/abbeydale-industrial-hamlet tel: 0114 272 2106
Abbeydale Road South, Sheffield S7 2QW
A water-powered toolworks used in the manufacture of knives, scythes and other tools. The 1830 Crucible Furnace at Abbeydale is the only one of its kind in the world which still survives intact. The 1785 Tilt Forge houses two huge tilt hammers, and the 1817 Grinding Hull had six water-powered grindstones and two glazing stones. Open daily except Friday & Saturday. Admission charge

Amberley Museum and Heritage Centre
www.amberleymuseum.co.uk tel: 01798 831370
Station Road, Amberley, Near Arundel, West Sussex BN18 9LT
This extensive museum site was once used as a major lime production facility. Chalk pits, lime kilns and associated buildings now form the backdrop to the story. The museum now includes a range of small working industrial buildings and workshops. Open daily Wednesday to Sundays. Admission charge.

Black Country Living Museum
www.bclm.com tel: 0121 520 8054
Tipton Road, Dudley DY1 4SQ
Recreation of a small Edwardian industrial town by the side of the Dudley Canal. Numerous shops, workshops and other premises rescued from sites across the area – including a working nail-maker's forge, an ancient beam engine and more on a 26-acre industrial site. Two single-deck trams of c.1920 and a 1909 double-deck open-topped Wolverhampton tram run on the 3'6" gauge tramway. Open daily March/April to October.

Finch Foundry
www.nationaltrust.org.uk › finch-foundry tel: 01837 840046
Sticklepath, Okehampton EX20 2NW
Housed in a former fulling mill, the last working water-powered forge in England supplied local needs for more than a century. It once produced 400 edge agricultural and domestic tools a day. The water-powered tilt hammer, drop hammer, and shear hammer are still operational. Some days, an artist blacksmith is at work. Open daily, March to October.

Forge Mill Needle Museum
www.forgemill.org.uk tel: 01527 62509
Needle Mill Lane, Redditch B98 8HY
Redditch once had several needle mills and produced 90% of the world's needles Forge Mill harks back to Victorian times when working conditions in the industry were very harsh indeed. Much of the original Victorian water powered machinery remains and can be seen working on Tuesday afternoons and at weekends. Open daily April to September with slightly reduced opening October to March.

Museum of Bath at Work
www.bath-at-work.org.uk tel: 01225 318348
Julian Rd, Bath BA1 2RH
This remarkable 'time capsule' of a museum, housed in a late eighteenth century former real tennis court, recreates, amongst other things, the shop, foundry and soft drinks businesses of J. B. Bowler & Sons, moved from their premises in Corn Street and faithfully reconstructed in the museum from photographs taken before the original premises were vacated. Open daily 10.30-5, April to September, and weekends October to March.

National Slate Museum
www.museumwales.ac.uk/410 tel: 029 2057 3700
Llanberis, Gwynedd LL55 4TY
The foundry at Dinorwic manufactured iron and brass tools and equipment

for the Welsh slate industry. From an engineering point of view, it claimed to be self sufficient, and able to make or repair any component part of every machine on site. The brass furnace is operated periodically. Check website for details.

Shepherd Wheel Workshop, Sheffield
www.simt.co.uk/shepherd-wheel-workshop tel: 0114 272 2106
Whiteley Woods, off Hangingwater Road, Sheffield S11 2YE
The museum includes a water wheel, two grinding hulls and water-powered grinding wheels, buffers and other equipment used in the finishing of steel cutlery and knives. There is a collection of tools and equipment on display in the grinding hulls. Reopened in 2012 after a Heritage Lottery funded upgrade, the museum offers regular demonstrations of the grinder's craft.

Weald & Downland Open Air Museum
www.wealddown.co.uk tel: 01243 811363
Singleton, Chichester, West Sussex PO18 0EU
A collection of more than 50 buildings, spanning more than 600 years, rescued from sites across southern England. The museum offers a range of demonstrations including blacksmithing, milling, pole-lathe turning and scything. Open daily from March to mid-December. Admission charge.

Wortley Top Forge
www.topforge.co.uk tel: 0114 281 7991
Forge Lane, Thurgoland, South Yorkshire S35 7DN
The oldest surviving Heavy Iron Forge in the World, the water-driven forge, in an early seventeenth-century building, was, from 1840 until 1908, used to forge wrought iron railway axles. It is preserved as it was in 1900. Three waterwheels in working order and the machinery includes hammers cranes. Open Sundays and Bank Holidays.

A LUST FOR LIME

Amberley Museum and Heritage Centre
www.amberleymuseum.co.uk tel: 01798 831370
Station Road, Amberley, Near Arundel, West Sussex BN18 9LT
This extensive museum site was once used as a major lime production facility. Chalk pits, lime kilns and associated buildings now form the backdrop to the story. There are several different design of kilns, the largest of which are the De Witt Kilns, originally with 18 chambers, which dominate part of the museum. Open Wednesday to Sundays. Admission charge.

Astley Hall
www.astleypark.co.uk 01257 515151
Astley Hall, Chorley PR7 1XA
The magnificent seventeenth-century Jacobean house, now a museum and art gallery, has some of the most lavishly ornate lime plasterwork in the country, dating from the 1600s – especially the Drawing Room and Great Hall ceilings. Open weekends, and Monday to Wednesday in school holidays. Admission charge.

Beadnell Lime Kins
Beadnell, Northumberland NE67 5BJ
Cared for by the National Trust, these eighteenth-century lime kilns on Beadnell harbour are viewable at any time. The Trust is also custodian of the Castle Point Lime Kilns on Holy Island – burnt lime from Lindisfarne was primarily used in agriculture.

Black Country Living Museum
www.bclm.co.uk tel: 0121 557 9643
Tipton Road, Dudley, West Midlands DY1 4SQ
This broad-based industrial museum contains are forges and other items relating to the local iron and steel industries. The lime kilns were built in 1842 and were in use until about 1926, The spur from the main Wolverhampton-Birmingham Canal was built especially to serve the lime works. Open daily, admission charge.

Blaenafon Ironworks
cadw.wales.gov.uk/daysout/blaenavonironworks tel: 01495 792615
North Street, Blaenavon NP4 9RN
Extensive remains of late eighteenth-century ironworks, expanded and developed in the nineteenth century. In 2000 Blaenavon was awarded World Heritage Site status for the industrial landscape including the Ironworks and the nearby Big Pit mining museum. The site includes furnaces, the impressive Balance Tower, workers cottages and a recreation of the workers' shop. Open daily, admission free.

Blists Hill Victorian Town
www.ironbridge.org.uk/our-attractions tel: 01952 435900
Coalbrookdale, Shropshire TF8 5UD
Blists Hill Victorian Town, one of the ten Ironbridge Gorge Museums, includes amongst its rescued industrial premises, a decorative plasterer's workshop, which has examples of moulded lime plasterwork, and there are occasional demonstrations of the plasterer's art.

Charlestown Lime Kilns
Charlestown, Fife
The limekilns were once part of an enormous late eighteenth-century industrial complex created by Lord Elgin. The fourteen stone-built kilns facing Charlestown harbour are currently under restoration. The exterior can be viewed from the roadside, and it is hoped that better access will be possible after the completion of the restoration project.

Imber Church
www.imberchurch.org.uk email: contactimber@virginmedia.com
Imber, Wiltshire (Imber does not have a postcode, Grid ref: ST965 485)
The mediaeval Imber church sits in the middle of the Salisbury Plain military training area, all that remains of the original village which was evacuated in 1943. The church is open to visitors on selected dates when the firing range is closed and inside the walls still carry their medieval lime plasterwork, with the addition of an annotated seventeenth-century bell peal, the best preserved in the country. Opening dates can be confirmed using the email address above.

Morwellham Quay
www.morwellham-quay.co.uk tel: 01822 832766
Morwellham, Tavistock, Devon PL19 8JL
Now part of the Cornwall and West Devon Mining Landscape World Heritage Site, and a major tourist attraction, the Quay includes the port, a copper mine, preserved lime kilns, and much more. Includes underground tours of the George and Charlotte copper mine to experience the conditions of Victorian miners. Open daily, admission charge.

Twyford Waterworks
www.twyfordwaterworks.co.uk tel: 01962 714716
Hazeley Road, Twyford, Hampshire SO21 1QA
Constructed between 1898 and 1935, this is a working waterworks which still contains much of the original equipment – including a 1914 triple expansion steam pumping engine by Hathorn Davey of Leeds. Also on site are the lime kilns, installed in 1903, which were central to Twyford's water softening system. Limited opening – check website for details.

Weald & Downland Open Air Museum
www.wealddown.co.uk tel: 01243 811363
Singleton, Chichester, West Sussex PO18 0EU
A collection of more than 50 buildings, spanning more than 600 years, rescued from sites across southern England, including workers' cottages, shops, farmhouses, barns, a watermill, and even a church. The museum also offers a programme of demonstrations and courses on techniques such as

lead working, stonemasonry, lime slaking and lime plastering. Open daily from March to mid December. Admission charge.

A NATION OF SHOPKEEPERS

Bank of England Museum
www.bankofengland.co.uk/museum tel: 020 3461 5545
Bartholomew Ln, London EC2R 8AH

Shopping depends on money, and housed within the Bank of England, the museum takes you through the history of the bank since its foundation in 1694 to its role today as the country's Central Bank, with exhibitions exploring the history of money, and examples of money through the past 300 years.

Beamish: The Living Museum of the North
www.beamish.org.uk tel: 0191 370 4000
Beamish, County Durham DH9 0RG

Huge open air museum includes recreated Victorian town with shops, railway, trams, Beamish Colliery engine house and pit yard. The 1855 colliery winding engine is steamed daily. Drift mine tour. Demonstrations of Victorian crafts includes such things as bread and cake making and making boiled sweets feature regularly. There is also an opportunity to see how a small local newspaper was printed. Check website for special events.

Black Country Living Museum
www.bclm.com tel: 0121 520 8054
Tipton Road, Dudley DY1 4SQ

Recreation of a small Edwardian industrial town by the side of the Dudley Canal. Numerous shops, workshops and other premises rescued from sites across the area on a 26-acre industrial site. Two single-deck trams of c.1920 and a 1909 double-deck open-topped Wolverhampton tram run on the 3'6" gauge tramway. Open daily March/April to October.

Blaenafon Ironworks
www. cadw.wales.gov.uk/daysout/blaenavonironworks tel: 01495 792615
North Street, Blaenavon NP4 9RN

In 2000 Blaenavon was awarded World Heritage Site status for the industrial landscape including the Ironworks and the nearby Big Pit. The site includes furnaces, the impressive Balance Tower, workers cottages and a recreation of the workers' shop. Open daily, admission free.

Blists Hill, Ironbridge Gorge Museums
www.ironbridge.org.uk/our-attractions tel: 01952 435900
Coalbrookdale, Shropshire TF8 5UD
Blists Hill Victorian town is a reconstructed Victorian working town, complete with shops, a bank and a public house and industrial premises rescued from elsewhere and re-erected on site. The shops are all staffed with well informed re-enactors, able to tell the stories of the businesses.

Cefn Coed Colliery Museum
www.cwmdulais.org.uk/cefncoed tel: 01639-750556
Crynant, Neath SA10 8SN
As well as being home to the largest horizontal duplex winding engine still working in Wales, the museum has the only surviving gas-powered tram on display, built in Lancaster in 1899 for Neath Corporation Tramways and powered by bottles of 'town gas' which were carried beneath the floor.

Glasgow Riverside Museum
www.glasgowmuseums.com/riverside tel: 0141 287 2720
100 Pointhouse Road, Glasgow G3 8RS
Built on the site of the former Pointhouse Shipyard, the museum collections include a large and unrivalled collection of Scottish-built cars and lorries, a recreation of an Edwardian Glasgow street, and a small subway station. Free admission.

Milestones Museum
www.hampshireculturaltrust.org.uk/milestones-museum tel: 01256 477766
Leisure Park, Churchill Way West, Basingstoke RG22 6PG
The Museum's collection includes recreated historic streets and shops, vintage vehicles, the Thornycroft Collection, trams, agricultural machinery and an Edwardian pub. Open Tuesday to Friday and Bank Holidays 10am until 4.45pm. Admission charge.

Museum of Brands
www.museumofbrands.com tel: 020 7243-9611
111 – 117 Lancaster Road, Notting Hill, London W11 1QT
Based on the world-famous Robert Opie Collection, the museum tells the fascinating story of the emergence of branding. Originally in Gloucester docks from 1984-2001 as The Museum of Packaging and Advertising, a second museum – Opie's Museum of Memories – opened at Wigan Pier in 1999, before the collections were moved to London to become The Museum of Brands in 2005, now containing more than 12,000 items.

Museum on The Mound
www.museumonthemound.com tel: 0131 243 5464
The Mound, Edinburgh EH1 1YZ
Based in the historic former headquarters of the Bank of Scotland, the museum tells the story of money. Art & design, technology, crime, trade and security all feature in the story of money and are included in the museum's story. Open Monday to Saturday, admission free.

National Museum of the Royal Navy Hartlepool
www.nmrn.org.uk/our-museums/national-museum-royal-navy-hartlepool
tel: 01429 860077 Maritime Ave, Hartlepool, Cleveland TS24 0XZ
Formerly known as the Hartlepool Maritime Experience, this is effectively three museums on the same site – Hartlepool Maritime Museum, the 1817 Mumbai-built HMS *Trincomalee* and former Humber ferry PS *Wingfield Castle* built In Hartlepool in 1934 by William Gray & Co, as was her sister PS *Tattershall Castle*. The recreated quayside contains the type of shops which would have been found near most eighteenth and nineteenth century docks.

Robert Smail's Printing Works
www.nts.org.uk/Property/robert-smails-printing-works tel: 0844 493 2259
7/9 High Street, Innerleithen, Peebles EH44 6HA
Preserved print works where visitors get a hands-on experience of composing, and demonstrations of printing. Presses still used today for commercial print jobs, including some of the National Trust for Scotland's own literature.

PHOTOGRAPHING THE INDUSTRIAL WORLD

Big Pit: National Coal Museum Wales
www.museumwales.ac.uk/en/bigpit tel: 029 2057 3650
Blaenafon, Torfaen NP4 9XP
Part of the Blaenafon World Heritage Site. Preserved mine with underground tours. Extensive site includes a recreation of a coal face with cutting equipment. Superb museum in miners' bathhouse tells the story of the South Wales coalfields. Admission free, but a charge for the car park.

Brunel's Royal Albert Bridge, Saltash
www.royalalbertbridge.co.uk
Saltash, Cornwall PL12 4EP
The best way to approach the bridge is by train into Saltash Station – the platform is just at the Cornish end of the bridge. Opened in 1859, the bridge spans the River Tamar, and can also be viewed from footpaths on both the Devon and Cornwall shores.

Clydebank Titan Crane
www.titanclydebank.com tel: 0141 562 2889
John Brown's Shipyard, Clydebank G81 1BF
The huge cantilevered crane is all that remains of the former John Brown shipyard where the great Cunard liners were built. A lift was installed a few years ago giving visitors access to the jib and amazing views over the river and its surroundings.

Crofton Pumping Station
www.croftonbeamengines.org tel: 01380 721279
Crofton, Marlborough, Wiltshire SN8 3DW
Built to pump water to the higher reaches of the Kennet and Avon Canal, the engine house has two beam engines, the older being an 1812 Boulton & Watt engine. The engines are regularly steamed, although the water pumps are now electrically driven.

Forth Railway Bridge
www.theforthbridges.org/forth-bridge/
South Queensferry, Lothian
The original railway bridge has now been joined by the Forth Road Bridge and the new Queensferry crossing. Viewpoint for all three bridges from South Queensferry. Opened in 1890, and awarded UNESCO World Heritage Site status in 2015.

Lacock Abbey
www.nationaltust.org.uk/lacock/ tel: 01249 730459
Lacock, Chippenham SN15 2LG
The birthplace of photography in Britain, and former home of photographic pioneer William Henry Fox Talbot. The abbey and village are in the care of the National Trust. The Fox Talbot Museum hosts regular exhibitions.

Museum of Science & Industry Manchester
www.mosi.org.uk tel: 0161 832 2244
Liverpool Road, Castlefield, Manchester M3 4FP
Housed in five listed buildings including Liverpool Road Station, the world's first passenger station, the museum covers a wide range of themes focusing on Manchester's contribution to science and industry. The six sections of the Revolution Manchester gallery explore Transport Revolutions, Computer Age, Engineering, Energy, Cottonopolis and the Structure of Matter.

National Science and Media Museum
www.scienceandmediamuseum.org.uk tel: 01274 202030
Pictureville, Bradford BD1 1NQ
Originally known as the National Museum of Photography, Film & Television, this is still the place to find out about the evolution of photography despite the museum's world-class collection of images having been transferred to the V&A (qv).

Swanage Railway
www.swanagerailway.co.uk tel: 01929 425800
Railway Station Approach, Swanage, Dorset BH19 1HB
Running 6 miles from Swanage, past Corfe Castle, to Norden, steam services are hauled by mainline locomotives and operate daily from late March to the end of October, plus special weekends and galas.

SS *Great Britain*
www.ssgreatbritain.org tel: 0117 926 0680
Great Western Dockyard, Gas Ferry Road, Bristol BS1 6TY
Brunel's great 1844 ship, the world's first propeller-driven passenger ship, was rebuilt from the hulk which returned to Bristol in 1970. The project was completed in 2005 and she is open to visitors daily.

Tees Transporter Bridge
www.middlesbrough.gov.uk tel: 01642 727265
Ferry Road, Middlesbrough TS2 1PL
The visitor centre promotes the history of the bridge and surrounding area, and tells the story of the industrial heritage of Middlesbrough. 'Walking the Beam' is an exhilerating experience. Open Monday–Saturday.

Tower Bridge Exhibition
www.towerbridge.org.uk tel: 020 7403 3761
Tower Bridge Road, London SE1 2UP
The exhibition describing how the bridge was built can be found in the south tower and along the upper walkway. Also open are the Victorian engine rooms below the road on the north side of the river, the engines beautifully restored. Open daily. Admission charge.

Victoria and Albert Museum
www.vam.ac.uk tel: 020 7942 2000
Cromwell Rd, London SW7 2RL
The recently redeveloped photography galleries in the museum are now home to one of the largest collection of historic photographs in the world, including the world-famous Royal Photographic Society Collection. Regular exhibitions on the subject are staged.

INDEX

Adhill & Company, Leeds 97
Amalgamated Anthracite Company 14
Amberley Museum & Heritage Centre 84-6, 101-4, 133, 135
Arkwright, Richard 16, 127, 131-2
Armstrong, Mitchell & Co 12-13
Arrol, Sir William & Co. 106-7, 118, 120-23
Aspinwall, Samuel and Thomas 129
Astley Hall, Chorley 83, 136

Baker, Benjamin 119
Bamforth & Company 31
Barnett, Son & Foster 67
Bath Brass Foundry & Iron Works 64-5
Beadnell Lime Kilns 79, 136
Beamish Living Museum 69, 96, 138
Bessemer, Henry 126
Beyer-Peacock, Gorton 111
Big Pit Mining Museum 110, 136
Black Country Living Museum 58-9, 69-71, 87-9, 95, 100, 134, 136
Blaenafon Ironworks 86, 136
Blake, William 7, 37
Blists Hill Victorian Town 69, 90, 98-100, 136
Bolton Steam Museum 46, 48-9, 129
Bolton Town Hall 34
Bond, William 129
Bouch, Thomas 117-9
Boulton & Watt 15, 141
Bourne, John Cooke 115-7
Bowler, J. B. & Sons 64-68, 134
Bradley, William 132
Bradshaw, George, Bradshaw's Railway Companion 34-5
Brown, John, Shipyard 122-3, 141
Bruce, Charles, Earl of Elgin 83, 87, 137
Brunel, Isambard Kingdom 63, 112-15

Cadbury, Richard 18-19
Caledonian MacBrayne 112
Caledonian Railway 34
Camp Coffee 105
Caphouse Colliery 8, 126
Carey, Evelyn George 119
Carnegie, Andrew 15
Cartwright & Sheldon 50
Cefn Coed Colliery Museum 14, 99, 125, 129
Charlestown Lime Kilns 80-81, 86-7, 137
Cilyrychen Lime Kilns 90-91
Clark, Dr. Thomas, & Clark Process, the 78-9
Claverton Pumping Station, 33
Cleveland Bridge & Engineering Co. 106-7
Clockmakers' Museum, The 128
Clovelly Lime Kilns 81
Clydebank Titan Crane 141
Coldharbour Mill 44, 52, 54-5, 130
Coleham Pumping Station 8, 124-5

Colonel Stephens Museum 31
Courtauld, Samuel 39
Crofton Pumping Station 23, 119, 141
Crompton, Samuel 44-5, 130

Dale, David 16-17, 126, 130
Danks, Fred, Ltd 14
Day, Summers & Co 75
Department Stores 99
De Witt, Hippolyte and De Witt Kilns 84-6, 135
Dick, Kerr & Co., Kilmarnock 66
Dickens, Charles Junior 97
Dinorwic/Dinorwig 20-21, 62-4, 126, 134
Disraeli, Benjamin 35
Dobcross Loom 42
Don Mill, Middleton 43
Dudley Canal 69, 87-9, 134, 138

East London Waterworks Company 78
Eastney Pumping Station 15
Easton Amos engines 10-11, 128
Elgin, Earl of 83, 87, 137
English Fine Cottons 57
Erghum, Ralph, Bishop of Salisbury, 27
Exeter Cathedral Clock 30

Factory Inspectorate 19
Fenton, Roger 115-7
Finch Foundry, Sticklepath 59-62, 134
Forge Mill Needle Museum 61, 71-3, 134
Forth Bridge 117-8, 141
Fowler, John 119
Fox, Thomas 130

Gasmotoren-Fabrik Deutz, Cologne 99
Gladstone, William Ewart 35
Glen & Ross, Glasgow 63
Gooder Lane Ironworks, Brighouse 132
Gordon, Alexander 107, 117
Grant, Janet and james 41
Great Western Railway 33-4
Greg, Samuel 16-17, 46
Griffin, Samuel of Bath 66, 68
Grindon, Leo H. 27
Guide Post Equitable Cooperative Society 97

Hall I'th Wood, Bolton 44
Harland & Wolff 118
Harling & Todd, Burnley 132
Harrison, John (clockmaker) 31, 33, 128-9
Harrison, John (mill-owner) 132
Hathorn Davey, Leeds 75-6, 137
Hereford Waterworks Museum 9, 21
Hetton Lime Kilns 81
House of Dun, The 82
Howarth, Richard & Co., Middleton 45, 47

Howlett, Robert 112-3
Hughes, George W. 104
Huntsman, Benjamin 125
Huron Expositor, The 27-8
Hutchinson & Hollingsworth looms 42

Imber, St. Giles Church 82, 137
Imperial International Exhibition 1909 40

Jacquard Looms 9, 46, 51
Jones, Rev. Calvert Richard 113
Joyce, J. B. & Company, 30

Kelham Island Museum 104-5, 125
Kennet & Avon Canal 23, 119
Knockando Woolmill 38-45, 130

Lacock Abbey 107, 109, 141
Leeds City Museum 33, 128
Le Gray, Gustave 111
Lever brothers 18
Liverpool & Manchester Railway 33
Llandybie Lime Kilns 90-91
London & North Western Railway 34
London & South Western Railway 35, 111
Ludlow, St. Laurence's Church Clock and Carillon, 31-2

Macdonald, Major-General Sir Hector 105
Massey, B. & G., Manchester 63
Masterton, George 93, 101, 105
McNaught, J. & W. 49
Medical Inspector of Factories 19
Morning Post, the 94-5
Mudd, James 111
Murdoch, William 133
Museum of Bath at Work 34, 64-8, 134
Museum of Science & Industry, Manchester 111, 126
MV Glen Sannox 112

Napoleon Bonaparte 93, 95
Nasmyth, James 63
National Cash Register Company 92-3
National Gas & Oil Engine Company 13
National Slate Museum 126, 134
Nesbitt, John 38-9
Nettleford, Joseph Henry 59
New Lanark 17, 126, 130
Northern Mill Engine Society 46, 50, 129
Northiam Station 31
North Norfolk Railway 31

Otto, Nikolaus August 66
Owen, Robert 17, 126, 130

Paradise Mill 50-51, 53, 130
Parry, Sir Hubert 7
Pennant, Thomas 83
Penson, Richard Kyrke 90-91
Platt Brothers & Co., Oldham 41, 43

Pollitt & Wigzell 52, 130
Port Sunlight 18
Potts, Edward 57
PS Waverley 120-21

Quarry Bank Mill, Styal 16, 46, 127, 131
Quendale Mill, Shetland 119, 127

Railway Inspectorate 19
Renshaw, W. E. 125
Richardson, Westgarth & Co 75
Rigby, William 63
RMS Olympic and RMS Titanic 69, 71, 118, 121
Robert Smail's Printing Works, Innerleithen 104, 140
Roberts, William 132
Robey & Company 15
Ross, Charles 71
Royal Albert Bridge, Saltash 114-5, 140
Rylands, John 49, 55

Salisbury Cathedral Clock 25, 28-9
Saltash Bridge 114-5, 140
Scott, Robert Falcon 128
Sheringham Station 31
Singer Sewing Machine Company 32
Smith, Adam 93-4
SS Great Britain 63, 113, 142
SS Great Eastern 112-13
Stanley Mills 16, 127
Stott Park Bobbin Mill 56-7
Swanage Railway 111, 142

Talbot, William Henry Fox 107-8, 113, 141
Tangwick Haa Museum, Eshaness, Shetland 72
Tangye Ltd. 125
Tay Bridge 118
Tees Transporter Bridge 106-7, 142
Telford, Thomas 6-7
Tenterden Station 31
Tower Bridge, London 12-13, 120-21, 123, 142
Trencherfield Mill, Wigan 13
Twyford Waterworks 74-79, 137

Valentine, James 117, 121
Verdant Works, Dundee 26, 47, 129
Victoria Sock-Knitting Machine 72
Vignoles, Charles Blacker 115-7

Walters, Mrs. 27-8
Watt, James 9, 13, 15, 63, 133
Wells Cathedral Clock 24-5, 29-30
Westinghouse Company 7, 21
Westonzoyland Pumping Station 14-15, 128
Whitchurch Silk Mill 36-7, 39, 133
Wilcocks, N. G. 64-5
Wilton Windmill 22-23, 128
Woolworth, F. W. & Co. Ltd. 98
Worsley Mesnes Company, Wigan 14
Worth Mackenzie engines 8
Worthington Simpson engines 125